THE ENTREPRENEURIAL EDUCATOR

Robert J. Brown
Jeffrey R. Cornwall

The Scarecrow Press, Inc.
A Scarecrow Education Book
Lanham, Maryland, and London
2000

SCARECROW PRESS, INC.

Published in the United States of America
by Scarecrow Press, Inc.
4720 Boston Way, Lanham, Maryland 20706
www.scarecrowpress.com

4 Pleydell Gardens, Folkestone
Kent CT20 2DN, England

Copyright © 2000 by Robert J. Brown and Jeffrey R. Cornwall

British Library Cataloguing in Publication Information Available

Library of Congress Cataloging-in-Publication Data

Brown, Robert J.
   The entrepreneurial educator / Robert J. Brown, Jeffrey R. Cornwall.
     p. cm.
   Includes bibliographical references and index.
   ISBN 0-8108-3883-4 (cloth : alk. paper) — ISBN 0-8108-3899-0 (pbk. :
alk. paper)
     1. Education—United States—Finance. 2. Educational leadership—United
States. 3. Entrepreneurship—United States. I. Cornwall, Jeffrey R. II. Title.
LB2825 .B72 2000
371.2'06—dc21   00-045022

♾™ The paper used in this publication meets the minimum requirements of
American National Standard for Information Sciences—Permanence of
Paper for Printed Library Materials, ANSI/NISO Z39.48-1992.
Manufactured in the United States of America.

CONTENTS

FOREWORD

Entrepreneurs create new businesses. Career professionals manage the education systems across America. The characteristics attributed to each of these professions are markedly different and there is no chance that one would mistakenly label a career professional an entrepreneur. At least there is no chance that individuals in business would make this mistake because business does not consider education a business.

Bob Brown and Jeff Cornwall begin this book by suggesting that business may be forced to reconsider its position on education if the trend toward privatizing public schools takes root and expands as anticipated. This trend is driven by entrepreneurs obsessed with the opportunity to demonstrate their ability to better educate the country's children. This obsession of business newcomers to education has been fueled by *Nation at Risk*, a U.S. Department of Education report published in the early 1980s, which calls for bold action to turn around the nation's failing school systems.

Chris Whittle, a successful publisher, is a good example of someone prompted to take action by accepting the challenge to produce a bold response. He launched Channel One, but his effort was bitterly opposed by national education organizations. These critics, however, failed to tame Whittle's commitment, determination, creativity, self-reliance, and motivation to excel. In the end, we all witnessed local education leaders ignoring the national organizations and embracing Whittle, helping him to create a successful new education business. Whittle's success paved the way for others outside of education, such as Steve Wilson, John Kim, and Doug Becker, to pursue their business ideas in education. These newcomers attract venture capital to education, and as they succeed others enter the arena, creating a momentum too large to ignore. It is the momentum of these business-oriented newcomers and what can be learned from them that appears to be the reason the authors tackled this subject.

The underlying premise of Brown and Cornwall's book seems to be that the only bad decision is no decision. The authors correctly point out that the public's demand for greater accountability regarding performance standards calls for bold steps. If those inside the system cannot, will not, or are too slow to act, they will be left behind by the growing number of outsiders who are excited by the challenge and willing to risk reputations and personal fortunes on their ability to understand and address important problems in education. All of this is a contextual framework the authors use as a basis for identifying new ideas and practices worthy of imitation. It is this very imitation that they hope will stimulate new venture creation from within the education establishment.

One refreshing aspect of this book is that the discussion of suggested ideas and practices avoids the fundamental attribution error of placing too much emphasis on the characteristics of individuals. It's what it *does* and not what it *is* that is important. People such as Chris Whittle are less important than the situation that creates them. Bob Brown and Jeff Cornwall rightfully focus on the situation and external forces that cause behavior, and use this focus as a basis for providing helpful suggestions to educators. They conclude that the situation dictates the need for more entrepreneurial behavior.

What resonates throughout this book is the authors' practical experience, direct approach to problem solving, and concern for the education establishment. The work does not glorify or overvalue entrepreneurs. It simply suggests that some behaviors are worth examining and possibly modeling if we are to succeed in building effective local learning communities.

—Dr. Joseph J. Scherer, vice president of Hifusion, the first significant
Internet service provider geared to students, parents, and teachers
*Dr. Scherer has also been the associate executive director of The
American Association of School Administrators, the executive director
of the National School Public Relations Association, and director of
Government Relations for the National PTA*

Part I

THE NEW REALITIES
OF EDUCATIONAL LEADERSHIP

①

HOW WE GOT HERE

Education is changing rapidly, but educational leadership has not kept pace. In the colonial era and in the early years of the United States, education was seen as a family and church responsibility. Primary education was provided in the home or in small schools, typically with a single teacher. As the nation expanded westward, common schools were stimulated by the Northwest Ordinance of 1787 and succeeding federal laws that provided land grants for the support of public education.

Through the efforts of Horace Mann and others, these common schools were merged into school systems by the mid-nineteenth century. Except for the elite few who would be going on to higher education, secondary education was not an option for most Americans until after the *Kalamazoo* court case in 1876. That Michigan Supreme Court decision clarified that it was legal to impose taxes to support public secondary schools. By the beginning of the twentieth century, public education was universally offered, although completion of secondary education did not become the norm until after World War II.

As school systems grew, so did their governing and administrative responsibilities. Common schools were governed by local boards that hired the teacher or teachers and then provided the general oversight for the school. With the development of larger schools and multiple building districts, the superintendency was established to provide general management and leadership for school systems. Because they often were the only ones in a school system with a college degree, early superintendents were seen as philosophers who gave direction to the system by virtue of their great educational background. When American business entered what became known as the "era of efficiency," school superintendents were expected to make the schools run at minimal cost. With the dramatic growth of school during the post–World War II baby boom era, the superintendency evolved into the role of a board's chief executive, with responsibilities for proposing policy initiatives and managing the enterprise.

Growth in the size of school buildings led to the need for designated leadership on site. Initially this meant the appointment of a teacher in charge or principal teacher. Eventually, as administrative duties expanded, the role of the building principal was created. This made principals middle managers in bureaucratic organizations. While they strove to be educational leaders, rules and close supervision by central office personnel limited the principal's ability to initiate action.

In recent years pressures have grown on all school administrators. Parents, supported by advocacy groups, are demanding more control over the education of their children. Since the 1970s the federal and state governments have required that schools deal with the long-neglected needs of special education students. In addition, schools must now provide special accommodations for a much larger group of students under Section 504 of the Rehabilitation Act of 1973. Low-income and minority groups feel that their educational needs are not being met. A rapidly growing population of limited English-speaking students also needs to be served.

Elected officials express frustration with perceived problems in student achievement despite long-term increases in educational expenditures that outpace the rate of inflation. Questions are raised about the lack of accountability systems that relate to student success. Taxpayer groups say that schools receive increasing tax revenue whether students learn or even complete their educational programs. Teacher organizations demand better pay and control over working conditions.

Responding to these pressures, policy makers and courts have been making changes in the education systems. Some of these actions are dramatically changing the face of American education and include the following:

1. *Limiting funding unless there is voter approval of education property tax levies.*   Beginning with the highly visible Proposition 13 in California, most states have imposed strict limits on the use of property taxes to support schools. The courts, legislatures, and citizen referenda have all played a role in limiting the use of property taxes. These limits reduce the authority and options for the school boards and administrators.

2. *Collective bargaining for public employees.*   At the same time as income sources are being curtailed, administrative authority over expenditures is

being limited by bargaining agreements. Master contracts also reduce administrative control over staff utilization and assignment.

3. *Making the school building rather than the district the unit of accountability.* The Kentucky Education Reform Act of 1990 was the first of many measures passed by state legislatures that held the building staff accountable for the success of students. These acts reduce the authority of the school district central offices and increase the responsibilities of the building administrators.

4. *Creating competition within the public school district.* Magnet schools, originally seen as a tool for desegregation, are becoming more popular as means of challenging schools to better meet the needs of their clients. School districts are creating alternative schools, particularly at the secondary level, at an accelerating pace. In Minnesota, for example, the number of students enrolled in alternative schools increased from 4,000 to 80,000 (about 10 percent of the public school enrollment in the state) in ten years.

5. *Expanding parental rights.* Individual parents now can play a significant role in the educational placement of the child. Advocates have taken these parental rights, which were clarified by special education court decisions and laws in the 1970s, and used them as the basis for many choice programs.

6. *Competition from outside the local school district.* During the 1990s, three reforms have created new competition for the traditional public and private schools. *Postsecondary educational options* allows students to enroll in college while completing high school, the college course being paid by state aid that would have gone to the school district (although some states allow for payment to both the college and the school district). *Open enrollment* allows students to attend any public school district in the state regardless of where they live. *Charter schools* are public schools that are freed of many of the rules governing other public schools.

Some of these trends are contradictory. The one thing they have in common is increased pressure on the educational leader to do more with fewer resources and reduced authority.

The trend toward greater accountability continues to grow. The demand for competition is increasing with every legislative session and every pronouncement of educational pundits. Demands for vouchers and tax credits, the growth of home schooling, the expansion of private education, and the development of for-profit schools are creating more competition for public schools.

Because of these changes and trends, the role of educational leaders must change if they are going to function effectively. Curriculum and instruction will continue to be the primary focus. However, now effective leaders must deal with recruiting students, acquiring resources, building internal and external community support, getting "more bang for the buck," and rethinking the very definition of a school. Most distinctions between the roles of public school, private school, and proprietary school leaders will disappear.

The purpose of this book is to help the educational leader rethink, redefine, and expand his or her role to meet the challenges of the educational marketplace. The next five chapters in part 1 take the reader through the steps needed to build an entrepreneurial education community. This will be done by defining entrepreneurship in education, contrasting the roles of the traditional leader with the educational entrepreneur, suggesting how to create an entrepreneurial culture and foster entrepreneurial thinking, and planning the implementation of the entrepreneurial education community.

Part 2 is more of a "tool kit" for the entrepreneurial educator. It provides specific information, skill development ideas, examples, and questions that will guide schools in competing in the education marketplace. At the end of each chapter is a list of suggested activities that might be tried and a list of resources for those who want a more in-depth knowledge of the subject.

Remember, this book is *not* a text on curriculum or on the internal management of the school or its personnel. It is assumed that the reader, likely a member of the school leadership team, has the appropriate background and knowledge in those areas. With that understanding, this book can be used in many ways. An entrepreneur starting a new school or taking over as the leader of an existing institution can use the book as a checklist for beginning the nonclassroom operations. The practicing administrator who needs help with a specific problem in dealing with the competitive environment of modern education can use the book as a reference for particular concerns as they arise. Colleges can use the book as a text in a principalship class or in a seminar on educational change or a class specifically on entrepreneurial education.

2

THE ROLE OF
ENTREPRENEURSHIP
IN EDUCATION

To many, the notion of applying entrepreneurial principles to school principals is a strange idea indeed. School administrators have been, and continue to be, trained to manage in a relatively unchanging world. They manage budgets, implement policy and procedure, and manage curricula. Change, if it exists, is incremental. As was discussed in the chapter 1, the administrator's world is no longer stable but, rather, is full of rapid and turbulent change. To adapt, the school administrator of today must become a leader who can navigate through changes that may involve the very structure of how education will be delivered in the future.

The well-known business management guru Peter Drucker has compared the world of education today with that of health care in the early 1980s. At that time, health care was moving from a very stable period to one of fundamental change. Managed care, newly emerging national for-profit companies, and rapidly rising costs forever changed health care. The typical health care administrator of that day was trained in a way similar to today's school administrators. However, as the changes of the 1980s began to take place, health care administrators had to learn a whole new set of skills to deal with such emerging factors as new competition, changing customer expectations, new funding mechanisms, and changing modes of health care delivery. The parallels to education today are indeed remarkable. When we described the content of this book to a retired school administrator, his only response was, "I'm glad I retired when I did." Yet health care has survived, and many of the administrators in health care learned to adapt to their new environment.

School leaders we have talked to say that they understand that their roles need to fundamentally change to effectively address the changes in education. However, many are at a loss as to how to accomplish such a transition and specifically how it will impact how they do their jobs. A common theme many of them hear over and over is that they have to become more entrepreneurial. But just what does that mean?

WHAT IS ENTREPRENEURSHIP?

Historically, entrepreneurs were thought to be born, not made. The word *entrepreneur* was used by many to describe a personality type. Entrepreneurs were viewed as high rollers who would risk everything on a whim. Entrepreneurs were seen as making and losing fortunes over and over with each new deal. The truth is that successful entrepreneurs are prudent risk takers who enter into new opportunities with a clear plan. Many focus on building long-term economic security for their families and their employees.

Entrepreneurs have also been viewed as lone rangers. Entrepreneurs were thought to be unable and unwilling to delegate any control or authority. They were seen as the antithesis to a team player. The truth is that successful entrepreneurs are those who understand the importance of developing a strong team. Much training for entrepreneurs is devoted to helping them learn how to evaluate what needs must be filled by their team and how to build that team.

The typical entrepreneur has also been portrayed as an extreme extrovert and just a little bit crazy. The truth is that entrepreneurs come in all personality types, and no type has proven to be more successful than any other. Entrepreneurs range from introverts to extroverts, from socially skilled to social-phobics, from outrageous to just plain ordinary.

The systematic study of entrepreneurship has demonstrated that entrepreneurship is a way of managing that can be learned by most managers and administrators. That is, entrepreneurship is what someone does, not what they are like based on some predisposed set of personality characteristics. Entrepreneurship is the process of successfully taking advantage of opportunities for the benefit of the stakeholders of an organization. These processes can be learned by almost any experienced manager or administrator. Successful entrepreneurs master a basic set of skills that includes the following:

1. *Recognizing change and the opportunities and threats it creates.* Successful entrepreneurs keep a sharp eye on their environment. They look for trends, disruptions in the status quo, or innovations that can create new opportunities. School leaders should pay close attention to broader trends, including those related to private schools, Internet education, home schooling, charter schools, education legislation, and changes in parental expectations. They should also pay attention to changes in their immediate environment in these same areas. We discuss this further in the next three chapters.

2. *Reacting proactively rather than reactively.* Entrepreneurs learn to react proactively rather than reactively to changes in their environments. Entrepreneurs learn to love change as they learn that change is the engine of new ideas and opportunities. For example, rather than passively wait for the expansion of home schooling to eventually have a significantly negative impact on enrollments and funding, an entrepreneurial school leader would spot the trend early and find ways to create an advantage for his or her school from this emerging trend. We explore this skill in more detail in the next chapter.

3. *Harnessing one's creative potential.* Reacting to change in the world around us requires creative solutions. All of us have creative potential, but many of us do not exercise it enough. This is particularly true for those in traditional administrative roles whose careers are built on their ability to manage predetermined budgets and to ensure that policies and procedures are adhered to. However, change creates situations that require school leaders to administrate less and to creatively problem solve more. School leaders must learn to effectively recognize and clearly define new problems and to use techniques such as brainstorming to generate potential solutions. They must learn to think outside the traditional boundaries of their administrative role.

4. *Understanding the difference between an idea and an opportunity.* Entrepreneurs take advantage of changes in their environment. Through the successful application of the previous three skills, many ideas will begin to surface. At this point, it becomes critical to learn to understand the difference between what at face value seems to be a good idea and what truly is a good opportunity. Is there truly a *market* for the idea they have developed? Is there a *margin* in their idea? That is, is it financially possible and sustainable? Finally, is it consistent with the mission of the organization? Effective feasibility analysis, which systematically answers these questions, will help increase the probability of success for any new endeavors by finding serious problems and flaws *before* significant resources are expended. Faced with the previous example of expanding home schooling, the school leader may come up with many interesting ideas to address the trend. Only some of these may be viable strategies for a given school district. This topic is examined further in chapter 5.

5. *Developing effective action plans.* Entrepreneurs are well aware of the importance of a well-constructed business plan. School leaders must utilize a similar approach through the development of action plans for new initiatives. This is a major topic of chapter 6.

6. *Understanding the difference between forecasts and budgets.* Budgets are financial tools that are based on what is known from the past. Forecasts require a different set of financial skills, as they are constructed for new ideas that likely have no history to draw on. These skill sets are also examined in more detail in chapter 6.

FORMS OF ENTREPRENEURSHIP

An *individual entrepreneur* is one who starts a new venture, be it a for-profit business or a nonprofit one. These individuals find a need in the marketplace, develop a plan on how to take advantage of that need, put together the necessary resources, and start up a new independent venture. For example, in education the individual entrepreneur could be the proprietor of a for-profit education management company. It could also be the founder of a nonprofit charter school.

The individual entrepreneur is what most people think of when they hear the term *entrepreneurship*. However, the process of entrepreneurship also takes place within existing organizations, and it is entrepreneurship within existing educational organizations, such as public school systems or traditional private schools, that this book focuses on.

Entrepreneurship can take two forms in existing organizations: intrapreneurship and entrepreneurial organization. Gifford Pinchot III (1985) defines an *intrapreneur* is an individual within a large organization who acts like an individual entrepreneur. The intrapreneur introduces new products or services that enable an organization to adapt to change and to grow. For example, the intrapreneur could be the unrelenting advocate within a public school system that tries to gain support for the development of an innovative alternative school for students with severe behavioral disorders that may not have been traditionally served within the school district.

Two important points about intrapreneurs need to be made at this point. First, the process that the intrapreneur follows is quite different than the one followed by the traditional individual entrepreneur discussed previously. Pinchot describes the intrapreneur as a heroic individual who, despite all odds, is able to fight the status quo and bureaucracy of the large organization and to champion the new product or service through the corporate gauntlet. The individual entrepreneur operates in the broader and more flexible economic marketplace. Each context creates unique advantages and disadvantages.

Second, intrapreneurship often takes place in organizations that stifle entrepreneurial activity. These organizations fail to create an environment that supports entrepreneurial behaviors. Intrapreneurs must find ways to succeed among people who are not able or even willing to help them succeed; or, as is often the case, they decide to leave the organization in frustration and develop their idea somewhere else. In the previous example, the intrapreneur might seek out a nonprofit or for-profit entity that is willing to support the opportunity they identified to serve behaviorally disordered children.

However, organizations can create environments that are relatively supportive of entrepreneurship in many ways. A growing body of theory and research shows that large organizations must support, encourage, and foster entrepreneurship to be successful over the long term in adapting to a changing environment. An organization that creates such an internal environment is what Cornwall and Perlman (1990) define as an *entrepreneurial organization*. It is important to make clear that the presence of intrapreneurs in an organization may not be a reflection of how entrepreneurial the organization is as a whole. Without support, intrapreneurs will, over time, leave for organizations that offer an entrepreneurial culture in which they can more easily and effectively pursue opportunities that they identify in the market.

The entrepreneurial organization is ready, willing, and able to adapt to a changing environment. Creating an entrepreneurial organization, especially within the educational arena, is not a simple process. It requires attention to the entire organization, to groups and teams within the organization, and to the intrapreneurs themselves. It requires paying more attention to the future than to the past. Imagine trying to drive a car while only looking into the rear-view mirror. The first curve in the road would most certainly spell disaster. Yet that is exactly what we do when we make decisions on the future of our educational systems based solely on how we have traditionally done things in the past.

ENTREPRENEURSHIP AND RISK

Entrepreneurship is associated with taking risk, and taking risk is a part of any decision making done in schools. The decision to build new facilities, to offer new courses, or to change the calendar or structure of the school day involves taking risk. The type of risk that this book focuses on is that risk inherent in the entrepreneurial process. The magnitude of this type of risk taking can be much greater in terms of both gains and losses. In a public school system, it is difficult to expect administrators to take on entrepreneurial risk without significant changes in how the system operates. Traditionally, there is little reward for taking entrepreneurial risks and succeeding, while there is significant personal and professional costs associated with taking such risks and failing. Also, administrators feel ill-prepared for pursuing risky endeavors.

However, in times of turbulent and rapid change, it is critical to remember that there are two types of entrepreneurial risk. The first type of risk involves pursuing a new product or service and having it fail. Dickson and Giglierano (1986) refer to this as *sinking-the-boat risk*. This is the type of risk that generally comes to mind when thinking about entrepreneurship. The ill-fated agreement between Education Alternatives, Inc., and the Baltimore City Public Schools is an example of an innovative initiative that failed. Failure in this case stemmed less from the quality of the opportunity and more from its implementation and execution. However, such a failure can create a chill over other school systems that are considering either implementing innovative solutions to pressing problems or pursuing opportunities created by change.

School systems, particularly public schools, have to be sensitive to sinking-the-boat risk. Failed risk taking can bring intense scrutiny by taxpayers and the media. Even though risk taking is necessary for a school system to adapt to change, media pressure can become intense. Unfortunately the press and to some extent the average taxpayer may have a short-term view that does not encompass the need to take risks in the face of major change and competition created by new educational entities.

Sinking the boat is a major risk for school systems to consider. However, it is only half the picture when looking at an educational organization and the entrepreneurial risk that it assumes.

Missing-the-boat risk is the second type of risk. This is the risk that defines attractive opportunities that have been overlooked, dismissed, or found too late. For example, several years ago the State of Minnesota founded the Minnesota Education Computing Consortium to develop educational software. Minnesota decided to spin this project off because it did not seem to fit with the state's traditional educational mission and because the state was unwilling to invest the money it needed to grow and develop new products. The consortium went on to become the original provider of software for Apple computers, which in turn went on to dominate schools nationwide. Clearly the Minnesota Department of Education missed this boat.

Organizations of all types tend to miss the boat for two reasons. First, they fail to identify new opportunities. Scanning the environment for opportunities is often not expected of managers and administrators in their jobs. It is also not a skill in which they have been trained. Second, opportunities are missed because although they were identified by the organization, it did not have processes in place to pursue the opportunity.

Entrepreneurial risk should be viewed as a balance of both sinking-the-boat and missing-the-boat risks. Ignoring either type of risk can result in the other type of risk creating disasters for an organization. School systems that seek to reduce the risk of pursuing new opportunities (sinking the boat) increase the risk of lost opportunities (missing the boat). Educational organizations that appear to be conservative risk avoiders really impose significant risk by missing potentially important opportunities. In times of rapid change in how education is being delivered, this could have a significant negative impact on the financial well-being of those organizations. Conversely, organizations that ignore the sinking-the-boat risk entirely become careless and risk financial ruin. There is a constant trade-off between the two types of risk.

Sinking-the-boat risk is reflected primarily in short-term performance. Budgets are protected, and no one takes undue professional risk. However, by increasing the missing-the-boat risk, educational organizations may negatively impact their intermediate and long-term performance. They risk being able to adapt to change at hand and may even risk surviving over the long term. For example, many institutions of higher education are investing in Internet-based distance learning, while some are not. Investments in technology that may squeeze some budgets in the short run likely will prosper or even dictate survival over the long run for these institutions.

INDIVIDUAL RISK AND CAREER ISSUES

In many situations, the individual administrators involved in entrepreneurial activities will take on significant risk themselves. Of course, this is not the risk of capital investment that an individual entrepreneur faces. In the case of the organizational entrepreneur, educational administrators risk their reputations and, in some cases, their careers on the new initiatives they are attempting to develop. In school systems that offer little or no support, this personal risk is so severe that administrators are generally unwilling to undertake entrepreneurial risk. The probability of downside risk for these administrators is great (i.e., career path dead end) and the probability of upside risk small (i.e., recognition for success, rewards, and promotions). This situation leads people who have innovative ideas for significant new initiatives or services either to forget them or to pursue them on their own outside the educational system that employs them.

Just as attempts are made to reduce the uncertainty of an educational organization, administrators attempt to reduce their own personal uncertainty and to assess the risk of being entrepreneurs within the organization. The organization can reduce the uncertainty of administrators by providing tangible support and by allowing mistakes. The outcome of administrators taking on too much risk associated with being entrepreneurial can be stressful. One of the most common coping mechanisms for this type of situation is avoidance.

Simply put, administrators avoid new projects and initiatives to avoid the stress they might encounter. However, administrators who can take on reasonable risk without a constant fear of their careers (lowered stress) will produce and pursue more new ideas for their organization. If administrators face too much personal uncertainty by being entrepreneurial, the level of missing-the-boat risk will go up significantly for the school system as fewer new initiatives and innovative projects are pursued.

Of course, a school system cannot totally eliminate the risk faced by an individual administrator, and administrators must be held accountable for their performance in new initiatives. Although some eggs must be broken to make an omelet, clear milestones must be established to evaluate progress, and the degree of failure that is considered reasonable and tolerable for a given new initiative must be clearly understood.

Entrepreneurial initiatives should not be reserved for administrators who appear more inclined to risk taking. Studies of entrepreneurial activity in for-profit corporations have found no difference in the propensity for risk taking between entrepreneurial managers and managers not involved in entrepreneurial ventures. Given the right opportunity and the right circumstances, most administrators can become involved in entrepreneurial activities within their educational system. It does not take an individual who is more willing to take chances. In fact, an administrator who is too willing to take chances may unduly increase sinking-the-boat risk for his or her employer.

The next four chapters explore the entrepreneurial education organization in more detail. Chapter 3 compares the environment in a traditional school system to that of an entrepreneurial system. Chapter 4 discusses the characteristics of an entrepreneurial culture in an organization and the process needed to create that culture. Chapter 5 discusses entrepreneurial thinking, and chapter 6 examines the process of putting entrepreneurial intentions into action.

REFERENCES

Cornwall, J., and Perlman, B. (1990). *Organizational entrepreneurship*. Homewood, Ill.: Irwin.

Dickson, P., and Giglierano, J. (1986). Missing the boat and sinking the boat: A conceptual model of entrepreneurial risk. *Journal of Marketing* 50:58–70.

Pinchot, G., III. (1985). *Intrapreneuring*. New York: Harper & Row.

Timmons, J. (1994). *New venture creation*. 4th ed. Boston: Irwin McGraw-Hill.

3

THE TRADITIONAL VERSUS THE ENTREPRENEURIAL EDUCATIONAL ORGANIZATION

The previous chapter explored how the concept of entrepreneurship applies to educational organizations. This chapter examines this further by presenting a comparison of the traditional educational organization and the entrepreneurial educational organization. This comparison simplifies what is in reality a much more complex set of issues. However, it is meant to provide an overview of the general changes that educational organizations must consider if they are to successfully foster entrepreneurial activity by their administrators and management to ensure that their educational systems will adapt to the rapidly changing environment facing education today. It is important not to oversimplify the dichotomy that table 3.1 seems to suggest. Instead, the characteristics in the table represent end points of continuums. Each educational system is facing a unique set of circumstances that requires careful consideration of the appropriate approach for a given environment.

For example, some regions and communities have more active development of charter schools, private schools, home schooling, and so forth. Schools and school districts in these geographic areas would benefit from becoming more like the pure entrepreneurial organization. In some regions, development is more limited, and only some change in these organizational characteristics may be necessary.

Table 3.1   Comparison of Traditional and Entrepreneurial Educational
             Organization

Organizational Characteristics	Traditional Educational Organization	Entrepreneurial Educational Organization
External environmental scanning	Identify threats to traditional and educational system.	Identify opportunities. Seek out change that can create new initiatives.
Strategy	Defensive protection of traditional educational system.	Proactively seeking new initiatives created by change and competition
Control systems	Budgets are only means of control.	Budgets used for short-term control. Forecasts and business plans used for entrepreneurial planning.
Structure	Formal lines of authority, centralized, and highly specialized.	Empowered staff that is willing to "do what it takes."
Communication	Formal lines of communication.	Informal communication that focuses on getting information to those who need it when they need it.
Creativity	Belongs only in the classroom.	Fostered and developed throughout the education system.
Organization culture	Serves to protect the traditional educational system.	Serves to support and foster innovation and entrepreneurship.

EXTERNAL ENVIRONMENTAL SCANNING

Educational organizations faced with the same environment often react to the same information quite differently. Administrators in different organizations scan their external environments for information in different ways. School leadership is faced with an overwhelming array of information. Any decision maker must develop tactics for selecting what information needs to be attended to. Decision makers in differing school systems will select different information for making decisions and can often interpret the same information in different ways. One school system may view the trend toward home schooling as an annoyance, while the next may see it as a source of opportunity to adapt to inevitable change.

Traditional educational organizations tend to be problem focused. They view their school systems from a very narrow and traditional perspective. Therefore, they do not pay attention to information that is not directly related to their narrow definition of their school systems and what it does for their stakeholders. As a result, opportunities for new initiatives (or, for that matter, reasons for abandoning old ways of operating) may be overlooked. Additionally, the very top management of the school system gathers most of the information that is used in decision making. Valuable information about trends and opportunities observed by others in the organization is ignored.

A narrow view of information in the external environment can result from an administrator's training and experience. University programs in educational administration typically do not train their students in the managerial skills required to deal effectively with rapid change. These programs, just as was seen in health care administration programs a decade ago, will need to make fundamental changes in curricula. One effective strategy will be to partner with business schools. Higher-education programs in health care were very slow to embrace change. As a result, they lost many potential students to MBA (master of business administration) programs that were better able to prepare health care administrators for the changes occurring in their industry. Eventually, graduate programs in health care administration realized that they must prepare their graduates for the new world of health care and transformed themselves. Health care organizations also began to realize that they needed to recruit managers from a much broader array of backgrounds, including those trained in marketing, finance, and entrepreneurship, to ensure that their organizations could identify and react to change in the market. It is likely that programs in education administration will need to implement the same types of changes in their training programs. If they do so proactively, they can avoid some of the problems experienced in health care administration training.

The entrepreneurial educational organization, on the other hand, tends to be opportunity oriented. Leaders in these organizations assess a much broader array of information from the external environment. Information is gathered from a variety of sources that include both the macroenvironment and the competitive environment.

Macroenvironment

The macroenvironment includes social, economic, political, and technological forces for change. The education sector in the United States and the school systems operating in this environment face a wide array of change within the macroenvironment.

1. *Societal forces.*   Social change can be both revolutionary and evolution-ary. Demographic changes are the easiest to identify and to plan for. Baby bulges and busts can be seen years in advance. Income and geographic trends also take years to unfold. Some educational systems have done a good job in identifying and planning for these trends. Others, as seen in some southern districts' slow reaction to migration patterns from north to south starting in the 1970s and 1980s, have not been as proactive in their planning. Subtle changes in lifestyles and values can be more difficult to identify and plan for. The shift to two-income households and the increase in single-parent families caught many schools by surprise. Others saw these changes and reacted aggressively by moving quickly to implement before- and after-school programs to better meet the needs of these new family structures. It is important to identify social trends early. The resurgence of private schools in many communities is the result of their being much quicker to address the changing needs of families since the 1980s.

2. *Economic forces.*   One of the most significant events of the 1990s was its sustained economic prosperity. During this time, many families became much more concerned about preparing their children to participate in the good economic times. In some school districts, the importance of these develop-ments were overlooked, and many private and charter schools took advantage of this by offering an array of programs geared not just toward basic education but also to prepare students for the ever expanding and rapidly globalizing economy. Programs with business components and language immersion have become extremely popular. However, all economic periods eventually come to an end, and so the entrepreneurial school administrator will pay close attention to economic changes and the resulting changes in education that will be needed to address the next "new economy."

3. *Political forces.*   The political environment of education has had two major "hot button" issues over the past several years. First, funding of educa-tion continues to stir debate at many levels of government and public policy making. A variety of funding issues surface during political debate, including the level of funding, vouchers for private schools, and funding for charter schools. The appropriate locus of government control of education has become the second, often highly politicized, political issue. It is important to remember that even at the macropolitical level, issues ebb and flow. Issues such as busing, student outcome assessment, and Title IX have had a major impact on educa-tion over the past twenty years. On a more basic level, general changes in po-litical attitudes can have an impact on education as well. Certainly, education feels the effects of these changes. However, as entrepreneurs in the private sec-tor have learned, opportunities also exist in seemingly negative political times. Those systems and institutions that are able to effectively and positively address

the political concerns being raised can arise to leadership roles and often reap the benefits of these changing attitudes. School systems that found creative and positive solutions to school integration in the 1960s and 1970s became national models and eventually grew in stature and gained support among their local educational peers and local politicians.

4. *Technological forces.* It is likely that no other force in the macroenvironment of education will have a greater impact than technology over the next few decades. Information technology is evolving so rapidly that it is difficult to accurately assess the speed and direction it will take over the coming years or even months. The increasing speed at which information is able to be processed, the convergence of various technological devices, and the creation of even smaller information processors will create a dizzying pace of change that will impact how we communicate and how we learn. The integration of cellular phones and the Internet and of computers, television, and telephones is well under way. The challenge to schools will be to effectively plan for these changes as they affect student and parent expectations. Yet private industry has found that keeping up with technology can become prohibitively expensive. Additionally, the issue of information "haves" and "have nots" will become an even greater concern in society. Education will inevitably be expected to help create solutions for this disparity.

Competitive Environment

Competition is not a factor that most education administrators think of on a daily basis. Historically, competition has been at most an occasional consideration that related mainly to private schools operating within their districts. However, as competition becomes a more significant force in education, administrators must integrate a consideration of competition into more aspects of their decision making. As entrepreneurs in the private sector can attest, each and every decision can create a competitive advantage or disadvantage in the marketplace. Therefore, entrepreneurs learn to evaluate each decision through the lens of competition.

Assessment of the competitive environment should be made with input from a variety of internal perspectives. It should include input from selected administrators, teachers, and parents who are active in the school system. A comprehensive assessment should be performed at the level of both the individual schools and the school system.

Assessment of the competitive environment should include the following steps:

1. *Identify all factors that are important to the customers*. It is difficult for administrators to think of the families they serve as customers, but since

families have increasing educational choices for their children, that is exactly what they have become. It is important to regularly assess customers to ensure that the list of factors is what is currently important in their decision on how to educate their children.

2. *Identify all competitors for students in the market.* It is important to keep in mind that district lines of the public school system generally do not define the market. Private schools often draw students from several public school districts. Also, if home schooling is at all a factor within the district, it should be included in the list of competitors. Any new competitors on the horizon, such as planned charter schools or new private schools under development, should also be included.

3. *Create a matrix that uses columns for each of the factors important to customers and rows for each of the competitors.* Also include columns for a description of each competitor, its basic mission, and its relative market share. Market share should represent the best estimate of the percentage of the total student population that this competitor serves within its defined market. For example, if a charter school serves only K–6, its share of the market should be based on the percentage of all K–6 students in the market that it serves.

4. *Make a realistic evaluation of each competitor for each competitive factor.* It is critical to be honest and accurate in this assessment. It is important not to over- or underestimate any competitor being assessed.

5. *Discuss the strengths and weaknesses of competitors.* Key decision makers in each school and in the school system should then actively discuss the relative strengths and weaknesses of the competitors shown in the competitive assessment.

6. *Identify trends in the competitive environment.* Why are certain competitors getting stronger? What are the key factors that are determining why customers are choosing these competitors? Are certain competitors becoming vulnerable?

7. *Reevaluate the competitive matrix.*

Assessment of the environment should be an ongoing process and not a periodic event. Therefore, the competitive matrix should be reevaluated at least once a year. Entrepreneurial school administrators learn to identify and monitor trends in their competitive environment along with all four areas of their macroenvironment. They integrate this information to develop a composite view of the context in which their school or school system will be operating. This information is then used as primary input into the development of the strategic and long-term plan established for their school system. Developing an entrepreneurial strategic approach is the topic of the next section.

STRATEGY

Once administrators gather information about the external environment, actions on that information are created through their strategies. In a traditional educational organization, information is used to reduce uncertainties and threats to its core programs. When an attempt is made to establish a charter school within a particular school district, such schools may be viewed by traditional administrators as a threat to their programs because of the direct impact on funding that they may have. Charter schools are viewed as a direct threat to student head count in the district, which in turn reduces state funding. Defensive strategies likely will be chosen by an administrator in a traditional school system. This could include direct attempts to block the charter schools and indirect attempts to block the schools through political contacts or by rallying teachers and even parents to oppose the new schools.

The problem with defensive strategies that are used to address major changes in the educational system, such as the growth in charter schools, is that they typically provide only short-term relief from the effects of the changes at hand. The school system may be successful in stopping the first charter school that tries to open within the district and maybe even the second. However, a trend, given enough momentum, inevitably wins out. The longer the trend builds momentum, the more strength it will have. In this example, then, the longer the school system fights the trend, the less likely it is that the school system can make the eventual introduction of a charter school in the school district into a positive outcome for the district.

An entrepreneurial school system takes a more proactive strategic approach to trends observed in the external environment. Change and competition are seen as sources of opportunities for new initiatives, programs, facilities, and services. That is, the entrepreneurial school administrator becomes a prospector actively seeking new opportunities. Information from the external environment becomes the raw material to help develop the vision and strategies of the entrepreneurial educational organization.

In the previous example, the entrepreneurial administrator would identify the trend toward more charter schools and begin to craft strategies in which charter schools can be a benefit to the school system. Rather than try to fight the tides of change, this administrator attempts to ride the change to where it is likely going and adapt to the changes it creates. For example, many rural charter schools in Minnesota were started as a reaction to the trend toward the consolidation of rural schools. Parents became dissatisfied with long bus rides for their children to communities many miles from their hometowns and with the loss of community connection that resulted from consolidation. However, school districts did not pay attention to growing parent concerns. Parents finally decided to use charter schools as a vehicle to re-create local schools in their home communities. The typical strategy by school administrators has been to fight these efforts. The entrepreneurial administrator would instead pay attention to growing parent concerns and find ways to work with them to meet both the concerns of parents and the school's needs to maintain enrollments. Playing an active role rather than an adversarial one in the charter school process might lead to a strategy that at least keeps these families partially connected to the school district.

Peter Drucker has identified four basic competitive strategies pursued by entrepreneurial organizations that apply to education organizations as well. These strategies are proactive and are designed to meet the changing needs of the customer rather than being defensive and simply countermoves made by competitors:

1. "Fustest with the Mostest." With this strategy, the organization attempts to be the first to pursue a new opportunity emerging in the marketplace. The goal is to be the first and to commit enough resources to dominate the market. Apple Computer used this strategy in the educational market in the 1980s. By giving computers away to schools, the company intended to preempt any other competitors and become the only significant firm in the educational personal computer market. "Fustest with the Mostest" is a strategy that is highly risky. Specifically, an organization greatly increases its sinking-the-boat risk discussed in chapter 2. Drucker compares this strategy to a moon shot. It takes a huge commitment of resources, and even minor errors in judgment can create catastrophic losses. Therefore, it is recommended that this strategy be used in only in the most unusual situations and only after careful and thorough evaluation.

2. "Hit Them Where They Ain't." Drucker describes the "Hit Them Where They Ain't" strategy, by which an organization observes another's attempt to start a new initiative and then uses the information it observes to do the same initiative, only better. The organization is able to learn from others' mistakes, thus reducing risk and start-up costs. The organization can gain knowledge about the new initiative from organizations both inside and outside its market. Many of the pioneering efforts in establishing charter schools have taken place in Minnesota. Important lessons can be learned by observing what these early start-ups did well and what they could have done better. These lessons can serve other new charter schools not only in Minnesota but across the country as well.

3. The market niche. Many entrepreneurs have discovered the significant advantage to gaining control of a small, often undiscovered or underserved segment (niche) in the market. The ultimate goal of the market niche strategy is not to be noticed, therefore not attracting competition. For example, a small private agency in the Southeast was able to identify an underserved population, namely, children with dually diagnosed severe behavioral disorders and mild developmental disabilities. The agency developed a program in one of its facilities to serve these children. This represented a fairly small number of children, but enough to make the program sustainable. These children were in need of more effective education combined with specialized treatment. The program proved to be financially successful and a safe niche with very little competition.

4. *Changing values and characteristics.* The final entrepreneurial strategy identified by Drucker has the entrepreneur searching for ways to make an old service have new value to the customer. For example, many schools no longer define themselves simply as traditional schools but also as sources of combined child care and education for families with no parent at home during the workday. Adding before- and after-school programs and serving breakfasts transformed these schools in a way that provided significant new value to their customers.

CONTROL SYSTEMS

Traditional educational organizations control the organization and in turn assess the effectiveness of their schools and the administrators who run them, primarily through budgetary management and implementation of established policies and procedures. Evaluation and control are based on comparisons to past performance and on historical fiscal data. As discussed previously, although important, this is controlling only short-term performance. Budget analyses tell only a part of the story of the organization's performance. They fail to evaluate entrepreneurial successes that are rarely evident in a given budget cycle but that likely will determine the ability of the organization to adapt to change and, in some cases, even to survive.

Entrepreneurial educational organizations must develop new criteria for their control systems that assess entrepreneurial effectiveness. The goal is to assess the appropriateness of the organization's entrepreneurial strategies and the success of its implementation. In the short and intermediate term, it is possible to assess only activities that lead to entrepreneurial initiatives. Only the entrepreneurial behaviors of administrators and other staff can be observed. Specifically, an entrepreneurial organization should have staff generating and proposing many new ideas. There should also be mechanisms and systems in place to effectively evaluate new ideas to determine whether they truly are opportunities. Periodic questionnaires and direct observation can be used to measure the rate of idea generation by the staff. The review process for proposed ideas should also be evaluated from time to time to ensure that it is effectively screening ideas and is still in line with the organization's strategic approach.

The long-term effectiveness of an entrepreneurial organization is based on its ability to adapt to and survive change. However, a school system cannot wait until historical data are available to evaluate these criteria, as by then it will be too late. To evaluate progress, administrators need to project the impact of new initiatives to assess the likely impact they will have on adaptation and survival. This is clearly more an art than a science. The administrator must gain a sense of how new initiatives position the organization for trends in the external environment. This will prove to be a moving target that will require readjustments to strategy as new information is gathered about the changing environment. During times of rapid and fundamental change, the entrepreneurial organization seems to constantly reinvent itself while still holding true to its values and core mission. Chapter 6 examines this process in more detail in its discussion of implementation and planning.

STRUCTURE

Structure is another organizational characteristic in which there are differences between traditional and entrepreneurial organizations. Highly centralized authority and decision making characterize the structure in traditional organizations. The structure is also highly formalized and is governed by formal rules and procedures. A well-functioning bureaucracy with highly specialized personnel is typical of a traditional organization. If the organization is operating in a relatively stable environment, as was the case in education for several decades, the type of structure found in a traditional organization is in fact preferable. This type of structure enhances the efficiency and effectiveness of the organization in its predictable and unchanging marketplace. However, the current environment of change and competition in education does not favor organizations that maintain their traditional organizational structures. Reacting to change requires being flexible and nimble, which is difficult at best with a traditional organizational structure.

Entrepreneurial organizations tend to have less centralized authority and decision making and therefore seek to empower their employees. As a result, they tend to have fewer layers in their organizational hierarchies. Cooperation and teams tend to characterize these organizations. Jobs are much less specialized, and this permits much greater flexibility, allowing administrators to react to changes in a timely, effective manner.

Teams are common within the structures of entrepreneurial organizations. Teams bring together a variety of people from various parts of the organization through which ideas are continually refined on the basis of new information. This is consistent with the adaptive management skills described previously in this chapter. The entrepreneurial educational organization fosters creativity everywhere and in everyone.

ORGANIZATIONAL CULTURE

The nature of the organizational culture is the final characteristic in which traditional and entrepreneurial organizations differ. Creating an entrepreneurial culture is an essential step toward fostering entrepreneurial activity within any organization. Chapter 4 examines organizational culture in detail and shows how it can be changed to become an entrepreneurial culture.

REFERENCES

Cornwall, J., and Perlman, B. (1990). *Organizational entrepreneurship*. Homewood, Ill.: Irwin.
Drucker, P. F. (1985). *Innovation and entrepreneurship*. New York: Harper & Row.
Timmons, J. (1994). *New venture creation*. 4th[th] ed. Boston: Irwin McGraw-Hill.

ways to "get by" were a hero, this would certainly be a clear indication of a fairly negative culture. Whom the organizational members consider to be a hero should be closely examined, as it will give a clear window into its culture.

7. Ethics. An important function of culture is to communicate what is considered right and wrong. Some ethical standards are written down in ethical codes, while others are unwritten norms that are learned over time. All the ethical standards, both those written and those understood though tradition, help define the core values of the organizational culture.

Assessing an organization's culture is not a quantifiable exercise, to say the least. It requires patient observation and an open mind. Through qualitative, unbiased assessment of the previously listed issues, a picture of an organization's culture should start to emerge. The following discussion focuses on the specific characteristics of an entrepreneurial organizational culture.

AN ENTREPRENEURIAL CULTURE

An entrepreneurial culture is one that supports the entrepreneurial activities of its members. It goes beyond simply tolerating innovation and entrepreneurship, and it even goes beyond merely encouraging such actions. An entrepreneurial culture is one that actively fosters, supports, and expects entrepreneurial activity. There is no single description that captures all organizations that have an entrepreneurial culture. Because cultures develop through the history and participation of its members, even entrepreneurial cultures can "look different" from each other in certain ways and still be alive with entrepreneurial activity. However, there are certain broad cultural characteristics that entrepreneurial organizations tend to have in common. These include the following:

1. Passion. Members of entrepreneurial organizations have a passion for what they do. They approach change and the opportunities it creates with enthusiasm and drive. Change is not viewed negatively but as a means to improvement. Passion is communicated openly and enthusiastically. Work is fun.

2. Vision. During times of transition and change, organizational members need a shared understanding of where the organization is headed and what it will look like when it gets there. This is vision. Vision includes an understanding of what the mission and focus of the organization is now and what it will become. Vision should be guided by the core values that make up the culture. Becoming more entrepreneurial does not mean that the core values must be radically changed or abandoned. If a school has had a commitment to excellence in education and an openness in how it operates, these values can and should continue to be a fundamental aspect of the culture, even as entrepreneurial activities help transform how the school interacts with its changing environment. An effective statement of vision should be clear, compelling, and enduring. Vision also defines how the organization treats employees and stakeholders. It provides context for decision making.

3. Risk. Taking chances, innovation, and new ideas are supported throughout the organization. It is understood that many new initiatives may not work as hoped for but that it takes such risk taking to achieve successes. Prudent risk taking that is carefully implemented is celebrated and rewarded whether it succeeds or not. In most traditional school cultures, risk taking is perceived as having limited upside rewards and unlimited downside personal risk for the employee. In an entrepreneurial culture, the employee knows how to evaluate an idea and how to take risk effectively. It is not a culture of "fear of failure" but one of "let's see what we can get done." The culture makes the prudent risk taker feel safe and secure in his or her actions.

4. Empowerment. In an entrepreneurial culture, members not only know what needs to change or what opportunities need to be pursued but are empowered to act on this knowledge. In fact, they understand that it is their responsibility to act. They feel no need to wait for permission.

5. Creativity. Entrepreneurial cultures become idea machines. Members feel free to express ideas without fear that they will be ridiculed or viewed as odd. Creativity is prized and can be found in many of the stories in the organization. Change is understood as the source of new opportunities and becomes the focus for new ideas.

6. Obsessed with success. Entrepreneurial cultures are characterized by members who are never satisfied with good enough but strive for excellence in every aspect of the organization. Success is measured not only in what we do today but also in how we prepare for tomorrow.

CHANGING CULTURE

Assume that the leadership of an educational organization has determined that their culture needs to be changed to create an environment for entrepreneurial activity. How do they go about changing culture? Clearly, culture cannot simply be changed by issuing a new directive or by setting up training sessions. One cannot order employees to become entrepreneurial through a memo or e-mail. However, even many larger business organizations, when deciding that they need to become more entrepreneurial, mistakenly try to take these types of approaches.

Changing culture is a difficult and long-term process. For-profit businesses have been trying to make the transition to a more entrepreneurial culture with mixed results. Those companies that have commitment from the very top of the organization and are willing to invest the time and attention needed to create real change have been successful. This is not a change that can be delegated, as culture starts at the top of the organization.

Changing culture requires a clear and honest understanding of where the culture is right now. A thorough assessment of the current culture is the critical first step in changing culture. It is also important to understand how the culture evolved to become the way it is. This includes getting to "know the ghosts" of past administrators and informal leaders who helped shape the culture. Changing culture also requires a very clear vision what the changed culture should look like.

Success in changing to a more entrepreneurial culture requires the development of a comprehensive plan. This plan should not be a written one that sits in a drawer or gathers dust on a shelf; rather, it should be a commitment to action. A plan for cultural change should include the following elements:

1. *Leadership.* The leadership of the school should have a relentless focus on the vision of where the school should be headed and on what culture is needed to get there. Leaders should provide inspiration for the school and be clear on their view of its potential. Leaders must also be prepared to serve as "emotional shock absorbers" for the distress caused by change. Even the most enthusiastic employees can become disheartened at times and lose focus. The leadership must remain outwardly positive and committed, especially when things get really tough. Leaders must maintain this outward confidence even during periods when they are experiencing their own doubts. Entrepreneurial leaders learn to adapt to unexpected change and learn from failures. They create clear objectives and milestones to help members assess progress. Finally, they lead by example to set ethical standards and expectations.

2. *Communication.* The leadership should provide consistent and frequent communication about the vision of where the organization is headed and what the culture must become to get there. In fact, this vision should be woven into all significant communications. Success agents of organizational change never miss an opportunity to remind employees of where the organization is headed. They always find a way to talk about the vision when answering questions and issuing new policies. The vision should be communicated to new and prospective employees during recruitment and orientation. A statement of the vision should be displayed prominently, even hung on the wall. It should be integrated into handbooks and personnel manuals and talked about in all organizational communications.

3. *Rewards.* Rewards can either foster or suppress innovation and entrepreneurial activity. To be effective, rewards should create the "upside" for administrators willing to take calculated risks that so many educational organizations lack. The criteria for evaluating performance should be expanded beyond the typical measures used in school systems. Innovation should also be evaluated. Innovations can be evaluated on the basis of their direct and their indirect benefits to the organization.

Direct benefits of innovation include both financial and nonfinancial outcomes. Financial benefits from innovative activities can include outcomes that enhance the school's revenue base. They also include initiatives that create more value, such as improved or expanded services for the same or even fewer budget dollars. Nonfinancial outcomes include initiatives that result in improved reputation or those that prepare for changes that will likely impact the school system in the future. Most of these outcomes likely will take time to be realized and observed, as new programs and initiatives generally do not reach their full potential within the first year.

Indirect benefits of innovation become more difficult to assess but are also important to recognize and reward. For example, even though some initiatives may fail, they may be judged as worthwhile if the initiative will likely result in future initiatives that will succeed because of what is learned from the failure. Another indirect benefit that can arise from failures is when the individuals in the team clearly learn skills that will improve their performance in future innovations. Very few educators are trained to engage in entrepreneurial activities. Some innovations will be breakthroughs that are truly unique. Therefore, some learning by doing must be expected, supported, and encouraged.

A reward system that includes recognition of entrepreneurial activity should do the following:

- Create a clear understanding that innovation is important
- Provide a means for frequent communication regarding performance for these activities
- Include a means for evaluating both short- and long-term benefits for innovations
- Provide a variety of incentives that can be tailored to the individual
- Be administered in such a way as to be perceived as fair

When compared to for-profit businesses, public school systems are more limited in what can be used to reward innovation. Even though schools typically cannot use large bonuses or raises as rewards, they do have many options that can be quite powerful. For example, administrators can utilize a portion of their discretionary expenditures, such as money to pay for conference attendance, to reward innovative activities. Evaluation criteria for promotions and merit pay can also be expanded to include innovation and entrepreneurial behaviors. Finally, never underestimate the power of public recognition. Awards can be created to recognize the "Entrepreneurial Staff Member of the Semester."

Over time, an effective reward system will help attract more innovative staff members. It will also help retain educational entrepreneurs already in the school system by making them feel valued and their contributions appreciated. Both of these outcomes will help the organization in its transition to a more entrepreneurial culture.

4. Criteria for recruitment. Many organizations wait too long to address one of the more important means of changing culture: recruitment. Most school systems have clearly defined systems for recruitment. Recruitment systems usually include specific criteria to evaluate new hires. These criteria have been shaped by the old culture. If the organization continues to bring in new members that fit the old culture, the old culture will not change. To help the process of changing culture, selection criteria should be modified to increase the number of employees that fit in with the desired new, more entrepreneurial culture. Criteria should be developed to assess potential employees on their ability and experience in pursuing new initiatives and/or creating an environment to support others in doing so. Potential staff should also be evaluated on their creativity, their knowledge of current trends in the overall education system, and their willingness to take calculated risk.

5. Structure. Chapter 3 presented a description of organizational structure in an entrepreneurial organization. Changing structure to more closely resemble an entrepreneurial organization will also help the process of changing the culture. Structure helps shape how staff members interact with one another. How staff interact helps define the norms and values that define culture. Therefore, moving to a structure that has fewer administrative layers, uses more teams, has less specialization, and allows more delegation of both responsibility and authority to where it is needed will support the process of changing culture.

6. Change physical artifacts of old culture—slowly. Research has clearly demonstrated, time and time again and in numerous contexts, that behaviors cause attitudes more than attitudes cause behaviors. Therefore, changing how members of a school system behave toward one another can affect how they think about one another and thus change the culture. In the example describing artifacts earlier in this chapter, the second school was described as a school where students attend classes but do not meet or talk with teachers outside of class and where teachers stick to their own offices. These actions were described as artifacts that indicate a rather impersonal and closed culture within the school. Assume that the goal is to change the culture in this school so that it resembles the culture of the first school in our example. In this school, students were seen moving freely in and out of teachers' offices throughout the day, parents were observed e-mailing teachers regularly to follow up on classroom activities of their children, and teachers were seen moving in and out of one another's offices and administrators' offices for informal discussions. It was described as a more open culture, and clearly it would be one that would support and foster entrepreneurial activity. The leaders of the school with the closed culture could shape behaviors to make it look more open through rewarding teachers, support staff, and administrators who interact more openly. Over time, the values behind these behaviors will become part of the culture and will become a self-sustaining part of the culture. Clearly, changing culture this way requires deliberate and consistent attention over a period of time and can be effective.

Changing culture requires deliberate action and takes time. Yet many school systems must make significant changes in their cultures to have any hope of fostering entrepreneurial activity that will sustain itself over time. Many organizations fail to take the time and effort necessary to truly change their culture. There is no one single change or intervention that will change organizational culture, as this requires attention to a variety of factors and can consume much of a leader's time.

The next chapter shifts focus from the organizational level, which has been the focus of the past three chapters, to the level of the individual "intrapreneur." The chapter explores how the individual intrapreneur thinks and what one has to do to be effective.

REFERENCES

Cornwall, J., and Perlman, B. (1990). *Organizational entrepreneurship*. Homewood, Ill.: Irwin.
Deal, T., and Kennedy, A. (1982). *Corporate cultures: The rites and rituals of corporate life*. Reading, Mass.: Addison-Wesley.

5

THE EDUCATIONAL INTRAPRENEUR

Entrepreneurial outcomes for an educational organization depend not only on an entrepreneurial culture but also on individuals who are willing to pursue opportunities for the good of the organization. Chapter 2 introduced the concept of the entrepreneur within an existing, often larger organization known as an intrapreneur. Now that we have the plan to create an entrepreneurial organization, our focus shifts to the individual intrapreneur within that environment. Remember that even in the most entrepreneurial culture, the entrepreneurial process requires hard work and dedication.

Although many people in an organization can become intrapreneurs, Pinchot (1985) identified a set of skills and attributes common to the most successful intrapreneurs. This section outlines these skills and attributes and applies them to educational intrapreneurs:

1. *Passion and commitment.* Successful intrapreneurs have a strong emotional commitment to the opportunity. An intrapreneur will talk about the opportunity as if it were his or her own business. This commitment will be even stronger for those intrapreneurs who are responsible for recognizing the opportunity in the first place. They came up with the idea, evaluated it to demonstrate that it was an opportunity, and advocated it inside their organization. They must commit a great deal of time, energy, and internal political capital to move the idea ahead. Therefore, an organization should avoid simply assigning an administrator to an entrepreneurial project and try to place the original champion in charge of the start-up process.

For example, a school system is developing a new, innovative model school in the district. Assigning an administrator on the basis of traditional criteria, such as seniority, will not be as effective as placing the original champion for the project in charge of the start-up. If that were not possible, for whatever reason, the school system would be best served by finding a leader with a true passion for the model being used in the school. Passion for the idea should win out over experience when choosing a leader for a new project.

2. Serve self and organization. Even in an entrepreneurial school system, there will be friction between the organization and its intrapreneurs. That is because successful intrapreneurs develop a dual loyalty. Although they are committed to the school system and its goals and understand that they are pursing their projects for the good of the school system in which they work, they are also incredibly loyal to their projects. Assume in the previous example that the school system decided that the new model school was not possible because of budgetary constraints. It is not unusual in this situation to see the intrapreneur try to find some other means to pursue the idea. The intrapreneur might pursue the same model school as a charter school or possibly as a private school. Intrapreneurs often coexist with the organization in a delicate balance. The organization must recognize this and understand that there will be times when the intrapreneur chooses self-interests over organizational interests. Such a choice should not be viewed negatively. It is simply an inevitable by-product of an entrepreneurial environment.

3. Team building. Successful intrapreneurs generally have the ability to build strong teams and work well with a variety of people inside and outside of the organization. As discussed earlier, it is a myth that entrepreneurs or intrapreneurs are loners.

4. Leadership. Successful intrapreneurs not only build strong teams but also have the ability to inspire their teams and create within the team the same passion and commitment for the project that they have. Successful intrapreneurs recognize what they are "good at," and it is often starting up a new project rather than managing it once it is operational. Therefore, they realize that to ensure the long-term viability of their project, they must begin to transfer control and responsibility to a team that can administer the project. Many successful intrapreneurs are "serial entrepreneurs" who move from start-up to start-up. The school system should recognize this and not try to lock this type of intrapreneur into a single project over the long term. Instead, this intrapreneur should be viewed as a catalyst for ongoing innovation.

5. Long-term perspective. Successful intrapreneurs are patient. They understand that it may take a long time before their ideas even begin to become accepted by the organization. However, they are doggedly persistent. Once the organization commits to the opportunity, it takes time to bring the idea to fruition. Budget cycles and competing organization demands will often slow down the start-up process, and, once operating, it often takes time before the anticipated outcomes are realized and the project becomes truly successful. Just as the individual entrepreneur may not realize profit for several months or even a few years, the intrapreneur must also wait for expected benefit to the organization to be realized with their project. An impulsive, impatient entrepreneur is rarely successful as an intrapreneur because time becomes his or her enemy.

6. Problem solvers. Since they often work with a great deal of autonomy, intrapreneurs must be good problem solvers. They are the ultimate experts for their projects. With almost full autonomy, they must be able to recognize and clearly define each problem they face, gather the information they need, and implement a solution. In start-ups, unanticipated problems are the norm, not the exception. The intrapreneur must be prepared to "put out many fires" and to try to prevent as many "fires" as possible. There will be many mistakes and setbacks along the way. Intrapreneurs understand how to learn from these mistakes in their problem solving. The intrapreneur must be able to help adapt an initiative if the original plans require significant change. In our new model school example, the intrapreneur likely will face problems with funding, construction, staffing, licensing, suppliers, community groups, and so forth. Successful intrapreneurs know where they are headed and do what is needed to take care of any barriers that get in the way. They also understand that a different route to the destination may be required.

7. Management skills. Intrapreneurs must be able to bring together the resources, support, and information needed to successfully implement their projects. Intrapreneurs are often managerial "generalists" and have a broad array of skills, including financial, organizational, and managerial (chapter 6 examines the specific financial skills required by entrepreneurial managers). Intrapreneurs also have strong marketing skills, which in this context means that they truly understand their market and their customers. Successful entrepreneurs in any setting learn how to "think like their customers." Chapter 6 discusses entrepreneurial marketing skills in more detail.

8. Communication skills. Successful intrapreneurs are generally excellent communicators. If the intrapreneur is the originator of the new initiative, the intrapreneur must be able to communicate the vision to the leadership of the school system. Intrapreneurs must be able to communicate the vision to team members and other stakeholders (both inside and outside of the school system) whose support is critical to a successful start-up. This often requires the ability to translate ideas into language that these different stakeholders will understand. In the new model school example, one can see how budget administrators may require a very different description of the new project than prospective parents. However, the commitment of both is critical.

9. *Tolerate risk and uncertainty.* Being an intrapreneur, even in the most entrepreneurial school system, has risks. Therefore, it is important to find intrapreneurs who can at least tolerate a moderate amount of risk and thrive on it. Intrapreneurs also must be able to tolerate uncertainty and ambiguity. New projects, particularly more innovative ones, will have a great deal of uncertainty associated with each step. This will create much ambiguity for the intrapreneur in all aspects of managing the start-up. Of course, some individuals are better than others are in handling uncertainty and ambiguity.

10. *Decision makers.* Intrapreneurs must be good decision makers. This can be particularly challenging since decisions often must be made without complete information. Educational intrapreneurs must be able to make decisions, at least in part, on the basis of intuition and experience. This can be difficult for some educational leaders who are more comfortable making decisions on the basis of established policies and procedures.

The preceding list can be used to help identify educational leaders who have the potential to be successful intrapreneurs. It is important to keep in mind that not every successful administrator will become a successful intrapreneur. Care must be taken to identify those administrators who would be comfortable with the "job description" carried by an intrapreneur.

The list describing successful intrapreneurs can also be used to identify training needs to increase the chance of success for intrapreneurs and their projects. For example, if an administrator were to come forward with the innovative school in the previous example, a critical next step would be to conduct a careful assessment of that administrator using the ten criteria in the list. If one or more criteria were determined to be a weakness for the administrator, such as problem solving and decision making, it would be important to try to develop a training plan that would help address the specific deficiencies. Some deficiencies may not be remedied through training. In that case, it would be important to add to the team developing the new idea a member who complements any deficient areas or to find another person to serve as the leader in charge of implementing the new project.

STAGES IN THE INTRAPRENEURIAL PROCESS

The intrapreneur typically goes through four stages in developing a new idea and moving it all the way through to implementation (Kanter, 1983; Cornwall and Perlman, 1990): (1) defining an opportunity, (2) coalition building, (3) mobilization and implementation, and (4) transition to successor. The skills and attributes discussed in the previous section will be required to successfully move a new project through each of these four stages of the intrapreneurial process. Therefore, it is important to plan out each new initiative carefully, making sure that everyone involved fully understands what will be required to successfully move the project from beginning through implementation and possibly beyond. Let's look at each step in detail:

1. *Defining an opportunity.* This first stage involves thinking like an entrepreneur. If the intrapreneur is the source of a new idea, he or she should spend time daydreaming and fact finding to make sure that the passion that is developing for the new idea is well founded. An important first step in evaluating the idea is to gather as much information as possible. This information typically comes from talking informally about the idea with people both inside and outside of the organization. Information should also be gathered from credible secondary sources. Since the idea itself is often novel, supporting secondary data may come from nontraditional sources. For example, since the emergence of for-profit educationally oriented businesses, much has been written about the future of education in various financial publications. These publications may provide very different insights than can be found in traditional education publications.

During this stage, the intrapreneur will take time to develop a specific description of the opportunity. Entrepreneurs in the private sector learn the importance of developing a "cocktail party" description of their venture. A cocktail party description is one that is about twenty-five words or less. When describing the idea to important stakeholders, the entrepreneur may only have thirty seconds to get someone's attention. Therefore, a concise description of the idea is critical. The description must be clear and compelling. It must leave no doubt as to the nature of the idea and why it is an opportunity.

To be a true opportunity, an idea must have a *market,* provide an adequate operating *margin,* and be consistent with the school system's *mission.* The intrapreneur must demonstrate the feasibility of the idea by making a case in all three of these areas. Demonstrating that a market exists for the idea means that the intrapreneur has gathered data that indicate that demand will exist for the new idea. Such data may be somewhat anecdotal at this stage, but it still must be compelling. Having evidence of potential strong support for a new initiative from informal surveys or interviews combined with supporting demographic data often is enough at this point. More extensive market research will be conducted through the action plan (see chapter 6).

The intrapreneur will also begin to develop the competitive strategy for the opportunity during this initial stage. Any one, or any combination, of the competitive strategies discussed in chapter 3 should be developed for the opportunity under consideration. The competitive strategy will also be developed further in the action plan.

2. Coalition building.   Intrapreneurs often need to build a strong coalition of support to ensure the successful implementation of their project. This is particularly true in larger school systems. Coalition building goes well beyond the development of the project team. The intrapreneur will need the cooperation and/or "blessing" of many different parties.

In our innovative new school example, the intrapreneur will need the blessing of various superiors in the school system. It may require several presentations to secure their support. Effective communication will be required to maintain support from top-level administration throughout the development of the project. The intrapreneur is responsible for keeping administration informed.

The intrapreneur will also need cooperation from various functional areas in the school system, including space planners, budget administrators, and curriculum staff, to name a few. If the school plans to draw from a variety of districts, there may also be the need to gain the support of the transportation staff. The more enthusiastic these people are, the better, as the intrapreneur may need to request new ways of "doing business" to make the idea work. The more entrepreneurial the organization is, the easier it is to build coalitions. However, it will always take deliberate action on the part of the intrapreneur to build the coalition and to keep the coalition intact. There will be setbacks in any new initiative. A strong, well-informed coalition of support will help keep any setbacks from becoming disastrous for the project.

3. Mobilization and implementation.   In this stage, the intrapreneur begins to mobilize the team, the coalition of supporters, and any other necessary resources to achieve a successful launch of the new initiative. Much of the implementation of the new project will be guided by the action plan (see chapter 6).

4. Transition to successor.   For many new initiatives, the intrapreneur may not be the person who administers the project over the longer term. The skills necessary to pursue the opportunity may not be the skills needed to maintain a healthy operation. Sometimes the intrapreneur recognizes this early on and sometimes not, which can lead to a painful and disruptive transition. That is why it is important that the transition in leadership be planned from the very beginning of any new initiative. Such planning often seems premature when it is not clear whether the new project even will be launched or, if it is, whether the project will succeed. However, experience from studies of private-sector entrepreneurs underscores the importance of building transition plans right into the initial action plans for any new project.

WHEN NEW INITIATIVES FAIL

No matter how carefully an organization plans its new projects, some initiatives will fail. In the private sector, an 80 percent success rate for new ventures is considered phenomenal. Failure can result from a sudden change in the external environment of a school system. The educational sector in the United States is in a state of flux that will last for many years to come. Sometimes trends that create opportunities can change dramatically with little warning. For example, funding for charter schools can be altered suddenly from one budget cycle to the next, creating either a sudden increase or a decrease in start-ups, depending on the nature of such a change. Failure can occur when the wrong decisions are made on how to address an opportunity. Such initiatives have school systems sailing in uncharted waters. As discussed in previous chapters, such is the risk of entrepreneurial management. Some failures occur because competition works its course, and the organization is one of the losers despite its best efforts.

Failure of a new venture in the private sector is easier to measure. If profit expectations are not achieved, a private-sector venture typically will be closed down. In the public and nonprofit sectors, failure may not be as easily recognized. Therefore, clear targets for performance must be established for new projects. These targets can include financial measures, enrollments, student outcomes, or other specific outcomes the school system is trying to address. Expectations should be established for milestone targets along the way as well. What do we expect to see after the first year? What do we expect to see after three years? Specific time lines should be established to monitor progress along the way to meet the ultimate expectations for the new initiative.

If the project is severely lagging in expected outcomes and the current trends show no sign of turning it around, the school system should be prepared to make the decision to terminate and dismantle the project. Once the decision is made to end an entrepreneurial initiative, the school system should move swiftly and decisively. Too often both the decision to terminate and the process of dismantling are dragged on too long. Decisive action will, over the long term, enhance credibility both inside and outside of the school system.

An entrepreneurial organization takes steps to protect the people involved in such a failure. The team answered the organization's challenge to be entrepreneurial. If everyone in the team did all they could within the bounds of what they could control, the *team* should not be viewed as a failure. To continue to foster an entrepreneurial culture, it is important that the team members be recognized for the effort they made. How failure is managed, particularly when failure is outside the control of the team leading the new project, will make a clear statement to other teams that are asked to take such risks on behalf of the organization. Also, there will be other new initiatives that the school system will need to pursue. Because of their experience, the team members will be an important resource to draw on to lead these new initiatives.

A major challenge of any educational organization is that its work is subject to the public's eye. Private-sector entrepreneurs do not face the same degree of scrutiny as do entrepreneurial educators. Although public scrutiny will be an issue throughout the entrepreneurial process, it can become a crisis when, not if, a failure occurs. Managing the public relations side of failure requires that several issues be carefully addressed:

1. *The school system's leadership should take pains to manage expectations from the very beginning.* One strategy that is mistakenly used to help build enthusiasm and gain support for funding is to engage in hyperbole about a new initiative. However, any exaggeration of potential outcomes will only create a public relations nightmare if the project fails. Be clear about the benefits of the new initiative, but be equally clear about the risks for its potential success. There is an old saying in the world of entrepreneurs: *Bankers don't like surprises.* The same can be said for the public. Do not oversell the benefits, and do not undersell the risks when communicating to the public.

2. *It is critical to communicate with the public throughout each step of the development of a new project.* A typical mistake is to play up the launch of a project and not follow up with information as the project is unfolding. Such updates can help build credibility, understanding, and support. They can also prepare the public by providing hard facts if a project begins to fail.

3. *The leadership must be consistent in their message on what the project is going to achieve and why.* There should be clear communication about the overall plan for the school system and how this particular project fits in. Talk about other initiatives and show the linkages with this project.

4. *Keep the message about the purpose of the project clearly couched in terms of both fiscal responsibility and concern for student outcomes.* That will provide a benchmark should failure occur with a specific project. The public will better understand what was expected, that this project did not meet expectations, and that the original goals are still important and will be addressed in some fashion.

5. *Continue to emphasize confidence in the overall plan.* This should be done, be it in the face of success or in the face of failure.

6. *Remember that the media will want to compartmentalize any situation and spin the story their own way.* The media may not pay attention to mundane progress along the way even if consistent communication is

provided to them. Find other ways to get the message out yourself. Newsletters, Web pages, e-mail updates, community and neighborhood meetings, and PTA meetings can provide a way for the school system to create ongoing communication about new initiatives.

This chapter has examined the individual intrapreneurs within an entrepreneurial educational organization. The next chapter presents a model to guide the development of an action plan to guide both the intrapreneur and the school system in the process of launching new projects.

REFERENCES

Cornwall, J., and Perlman, B. (1990). *Organizational entrepreneurship*. Homewood, Ill.: Irwin.
Drucker, P. (1985). *Innovation and entrepreneurship*. New York: Harper & Row.
Kantor, R. (1983). *The change masters*. New York: Simon & Schuster.
Pinchot, G., III. (1985). *Intrapreneuring*. New York: Harper & Row.

6

PLANNING AND
IMPLEMENTATION OF THE
ENTREPRENEURIAL COMMUNITY

The first five chapters have described the conditions that create the current need for entrepreneurship in educational administration, the changes that must take place in an educational system or organization before it can successfully foster entrepreneurship, and what individual intrapreneurs face in their endeavors. This chapter presents a model for developing an action plan that will help guide the planning and implementation of new entrepreneurial education initiatives and improve their chances for success.

Developing an action plan serves four important purposes. First, it provides the detailed road map for a new project and the new project team. The entire start-up team should participate in the development of the action plan if at all possible. This will ensure that the entire team shares a sense of ownership. Second, the plan can serve as a means of communication about the new project to constituencies both inside and outside of the project team. It will help build the coalition discussed in the previous chapter. Third, the plan can be used to help recruit people to the project team. Finally, it can help point out serious problems with the project before a large amount of resources is committed. Some problems in the project plan can be proactively pursued and corrected in the planning stage. Others may be fatal flaws that indicate that the project should be terminated even before it begins. Entrepreneurs call this "learning to fail on paper."

The action plan in this chapter closely parallels the business plan used by private-sector entrepreneurs. A suggested outline for the action plan is as follows:

1. *Executive summary*. Provides a complete synopsis of the project
2. *Mission of the project*. Clearly states the purpose of the project, where it

will be delivered, and whom it will serve; also provides an outline of the desired organizational culture

3. *Rationale*. Presents the external factors that are the source for the opportunity; should include trends, facts, and data taken from local, regional, and national perspectives

4. *Marketing plan*. Includes an analysis of the competition, the results of market research, a description of how the project will fit in the market, and a promotional plan

5. *Operating plan*. Includes consideration of space and staffing needs; also presents basic information on how the project will be managed

6. *The team*. Should list known members of the start-up team and descriptions of the type of people who will need to be added to the team

7. *Financial plan*. Displays financial projections and the assumptions used to create those projections

The following sections present the steps in developing an action plan. As will be seen, the plan should be developed in an order that is different from the order it is presented in the final document. Using the steps outlined here will help create an action plan that is internally consistent. If fundamental inconsistencies arise, the project should be changed or abandoned, depending on the nature of the inconsistency.

STEP 1: MISSION AND RATIONALE

The planning process should begin with a clear statement of purpose. This statement of purpose will come out of the leaders' vision for the project. For the purposes of the action plan, it should be structured as a mission statement. The mission statement should (1) be a clear statement of what the educational venture is going to be, (2) define who it is intended to serve, and (3) identify where it is going to operate. The mission statement takes the leadership's vision and brings it into the here and now. It goes beyond the cocktail party description discussed earlier and provides a more clearly defined statement of the project. A description of the desired characteristics of the organizational culture should also be outlined.

A charter school being planned in St. Paul, Minnesota, provides a good example of a mission statement:

ACADEMIA CESAR CHAVEZ is dedicated to providing a quality education for Hispanic youth and their families in St. Paul that prepares critically thinking, socially competent, values driven, and culturally aware learners by utilizing Latino cultural values in an environment of "familia" and community.

The rationale for a new project describes the source of the opportunity. It presents the external factors that created the need for the project, including trends, facts, and data taken from local, regional, and national perspectives. This information should have been developed during the first stage of the intrapreneurial process described in the previous chapter. Intrapreneurs should be trained to immediately begin to assess whether their ideas are opportunities. This should be accompanied by scanning for information supporting that there is demand for their idea.

In the example of the St. Paul charter school for Hispanic youth, supporting rationale came from a variety of sources. A sample of the information that supported the development of the school included a growth in the Latino population in St. Paul, local and state support for new charter schools, an increasing number of willing sponsors for charter schools, and strong demand for other educational services focusing on the Latino community in St. Paul.

A summary of all critical information should be incorporated to build support for the opportunity. Depending on the audience, the rationale section of the plan may actually be fairly short. If the audience is very familiar with the rationale for the new project, a tightly written summary of up to two pages should suffice. The information should still be included, as it will serve as a reminder of the project's rationale and purpose to all involved. There likely will be a time in the near future when the team will need to be reminded as to why they are all working so hard and taking risks. If other stakeholders are going to read the plan, a somewhat longer version with a little more detail or explanation would be justified. However, the presentation should still be kept to no more than five pages.

STEP 2: MARKETING PLAN

Marketing is a negative term to some in the field of education. It conjures up images of slick messages used at the expense of the actual quality of educational services. To some, it represents a cheapening of education, turning parents and children into customers and education into a commodity.

However, marketing is simply a tool, and it is a tool that is being used effectively by the growing number of private and semipublic educational systems competing with one another and with public school systems for enrollments. Competition may be a distasteful notion to many in public education, but it is increasingly a reality. Successfully competing in such an environment requires that public and traditional private school systems develop the capacity to engage in marketing.

Marketing is much more than simply advertising. Marketing is the development of a competitive strategy using what is known as the "Four Ps":

1. Product.   Offering the right set of educational services for the marketplace is the goal of this part of marketing. Those trained in education typically view the definition of the "product" they offer quite narrowly. In fact, product includes all that incorporates the experience of gaining an education in a school. *Product* for a school system includes not only curriculum offerings but also all the other criteria that parents use in making a choice of schools. This can include faculty, extracurricular options, reputation for placement in higher education, safety, child care, food service, facilities, and so forth.

2. Price.   In education, parents look at value, which is the ratio of perceived quality over cost. Parents are willing to pay more for an education if they perceive that it is of superior quality. Although public school systems have an inherent price advantage (i.e., public education is free), parents will choose to pay a higher price if they perceive the quality of private education to be significantly better, thus yielding a greater value.

3. Place.   Thirty years ago, the term *place* in education would simply refer to the physical location of a school building. Although the location of a school building is still important in terms of convenience and safety, it is no longer the only consideration. The options for place in education now transcend the school building. Home schooling, Internet education, and experientially based internship programs are just some examples of new options for what can be considered a classroom.

4. Promotion.   Advertising and promotion are what most people think of as marketing. Indeed, promotion is a key part of marketing. However, as can be seen in the previous list, it is only one part of an effective marketing plan. The goal of promotion is finding effective means to communicate with customers and potential customers about your product. The message should address the criteria parents consider important in making their choice in schools. The message should be contained in media that will reach them most effectively.

The objective of the marketing plan is to develop the strategy for addressing each of the "Four Ps." The foundation for the marketing plan was laid during the first stage of the intrapreneurial process. The task now is to go into much more detail in each area. A typical marketing plan includes the following sections:

1. Competitive analysis.   The first step in creating an effective marketing plan is a thorough understanding of "the competition." This step is critical to developing strategies for product, pricing, place, and promotion. A complete analysis of the competitive environment requires accurate market research. To compete effectively, a school system must have accurate data on what criteria are most important to parents making a decision on where to send their children to school. As part of the competitive analysis, market research should be conducted through surveys or focus group interviews to assess what criteria parents are using for their choice in schools within the school system's "market area." This research should also assess the parents' perception of the quality of the public school system and other competitors for each of these criteria.

For example, market research may find that for middle-class parents in the district, safety, college admission success, quality of sports programs, and accessibility of teachers to students and parents are the most important criteria in their choice of schools. Each school or other educational alternative (e.g., home schooling) that draws students in that district should be evaluated on the basis of the most important criteria. The best way to organize these data for the action plan is by using a competitive analysis matrix, which is shown in figure 6.1. On the basis of an objective evaluation, each of the schools in the matrix should be evaluated on their respective quality using each of the identified criteria.

Criteria vary between parents within the same district, so 100 percent market share (i.e., all possible students in the market) is unrealistic. However, it is important to identify the various diverse segments of the local market and perform a competitive analysis for each. An estimate of the total size of each market segment (total number of potential students) should be derived from available public data sources. From this, a realistic goal for market share (percentage of total market) can be determined. A forecast for enrollments is then calculated by taking market share times total market for each segment. In a start-up, it is wise to assume that full enrollment will not be attained during

	Safety	College	Prep Sports	Access to Teachers
Public School				
Private School				
Charter School				
Home Schooling				

Figure 6.1   Sample Competitive Analysis Matrix for a School District

the first year unless there are compelling data to indicate that such enrollments are possible. A three-year ramp up to maximum projected enrollments is not an unrealistic assumption for growth.

2. Market positioning.   Not every school can serve every family. Therefore, the school system should determine which segment, or segments, of the market it can best serve given the constraints it faces (e.g., facilities, mission, budget, and statutory limitations). Public school systems typically have tried to serve the market as if it is homogeneous in its needs. However, markets are diverse and may require different services for the different segments. The action plan should include an accurate assessment of the total size of the market and of each segment within that market. Clearly, many of the charter schools that are emerging are the result of segments of the population that believe that traditional public schools, as they have been historically operated, do not meet the criteria that are important for these parents in their school choice. Once a decision is made regarding the segments of the market, competitive strategies should be developed for each segment (see chapter 3). All of this should then be included within the action plan.

3. Promotional plan.   Much of what drives a competitive educational environment is the information that parents have at their disposal. The school system and its competitors are in a battle to mold the perceptions of the parents within this environment. Public and established private schools have not had to worry about promoting what is good about their schools in the past. With competition, all that changes.

The competitive analysis and market research provide a clear picture of what is important to parents in their school choice. Established schools should use what they have learned from this information and find effective methods to communicate what makes their school better. An old marketing adage is, "Think like the customer." The school must learn how the parents gather information to make their decisions and make sure that the information the school wants to communicate is effectively delivered within that context. A good example can be seen in higher education. Over the past few years, parents and high school students have relied more and more on the Internet to gather information about colleges. Colleges that have recognized this trend in how parents and students gather information and that have found effective ways to get their "message out" through this new medium can have a distinct competitive advantage.

The action plan should include a well-developed promotional plan. The promotional plan should identify the message that needs to be communicated, media that best deliver that message to parents, and a clear budget to implement that plan—and remember, think like a "customer."

STEP 3: REVENUE PLAN

Much of what is known about available revenues from year to year is derived from the traditional budgeting process. However, budgets are historically based. As new initiatives are developed within the school system, an alternative method for estimating revenues may be required. (Note that expenses are not developed in detail until Step 5.) For new educational ventures, revenues cannot be derived from last year's figures because if there even was a last year, it may not be a good predictor of this year because of continued growth or changes in the competitive market.

Many entrepreneurs (of all types) make a critical and often fatal mistake at this point in their planning. Our training in traditional budgeting teaches us to spend most of our time estimating expenses that will be required to run the organization. In fact, it has been demonstrated that left to their own, most entrepreneurs will spend at least 80 percent of the time massaging and modeling the various categories of expenses and less than 20 percent of the time estimating revenues. In fact, many entrepreneurs will simply estimate revenues on the basis of the expenses they anticipate spending. However, accuracy in revenue forecasts is what more often makes or breaks an entrepreneurial venture of any type. If one assumes a level of revenues based on very little systematic thought and then makes commitments for spending based on those revenue projections, disaster can occur if those revenue estimates do not materialize.

Constructing revenue forecasts for a new initiative should begin with the information developed in the marketing plan (Step 2). By looking at the structure of the market, the plans to attract segments of the market to the school system's array of programs, and reasonable estimates of market share, a realistic revenue forecast can be determined. Forecasts should be made for several time periods into the future (at least three years and preferably five) to accurately model anticipated growth in enrollments over time. To develop accurate forecasts of revenues, many entrepreneurs find that they spend 80 percent of their time on *revenue estimates* and only 20 percent estimating expenses.

Another key component of forecasting is to create an inventory of the major assumptions used to make the revenue forecasts. In establishing forecasts, assumptions will have to be made. Each time a major assumption is made, it should be documented. The list of assumptions will then help serve as a control mechanism as the initiative develops. The leaders should frequently test the assumptions that were made. If key assumptions were not correct, the forecasts should be immediately adjusted to determine the potential financial impact so that any necessary corrective actions can be made quickly and decisively. For example, the model may assume a certain level of funding per pupil and a certain class size. If the funding level turns out to be less than antici-pated because of the state's ever changing political climate, then expenses may need to be adjusted to reflect the decrease in actual revenues versus those forecasted. On the other hand, if the leadership observes that the new initia-tive can support larger class sizes than originally assumed, previously cut ex-penses may be able to be restored because of higher revenues. This demon-strates why leading a start-up educational venture requires a management style that is both highly focused (a tight watch on the key assumptions) and flexible (readily adaptable to changing conditions).

Cooperation from the financial and accounting units of the system will be necessary to get the needed data to track key assumptions. New numbers may be required, and they may be required more often than the system is accus-tomed to producing. This is where the development by the intrapreneur of key support within the organization is critical, as was discussed in chapter 5.

The final component of the financial plan is the list of key milestones and measures of success during start-up and growth. For each key milestone, such as opening day or end of the first term, predetermined measures for success to that point should be evaluated. In addition to monitoring assumptions, mea-sures of success at key milestones will be the other key tool to allow for "mid-course corrections" for the project.

STEP 4: OPERATING AND TEAM PLANS

Most school administrators are well trained in the development of operating plans, which is the next step in the development of the action plan. A detailed description of all space and resource needs should be included. Resources might include special computer software and hardware, special equipment, and unusual library resources, in addition to any standard equipment needs.

Part of the operating plan includes the development of policies and proce-dures. Certainly established policies and procedures from existing schools in the system can serve as a starting point. However, this portion of the operating plan should be tailored to fit the specific nature of any new initiative and, most important, the culture that the leadership wishes to instill within the new pro-gram. Therefore, each policy and procedure should be carefully measured against the vision and desired culture of the new initiative.

Specific plans for organizational structure should be outlined in this portion of the action plan. Also, any specific governance plans should be described.

Staffing plans will need to be carefully tied to anticipated patterns of growth established in the revenue forecast model and the marketing plan. Staffing plans should also reflect the desired culture and vision of the initiative being planned. Growth in teaching, support, and administrative staff should all be tied to specific revenue and size targets. These targets should be points at which increased revenues can in fact cover the new staff expense. Communication of the staffing plan is important, as existing staff may become somewhat stretched until the next level of staff is added. Assurance that help will be on its way at a specific juncture should reduce the distress caused by these growing pains.

The team plan should have two basic components. First, it should include a brief description of known team members, including their role and qualifications, and a description of any specific team members who will need to be added for the start-up. Second, it should include a team development plan. As discussed in chapter 5, this should include any transition plans anticipated for the leadership of the new project over time.

STEP 5: EXPENSES PLAN

At this point in the development of the action plan, the leadership should return to the financial plan to develop the expense portion of their forecasts in detail. Expenses should be forecast for three to five years to correspond to the revenue forecasts that were already established in Step 3. The fully developed marketing and operating plans can provide much of the detail. Recall what was stated previously: You should allocate only about 20 percent of time to developing the financial forecasts to expenses. Experienced educators should be able to create accurate expense forecasts in a relatively short amount of time. These forecasts should *not* be used for budgetary management. Actual budgeting should be a separate process tied to traditional financial control systems. However, start-ups should not be tightly managed by each expense category even in the budgetary system. Budget review should take into account the uncertainty of such a project and allow for flexibility in creating a balanced budget overall.

If the revenue forecasts developed in Step 3 do not result in a balanced budget at this point, the expenses should be adjusted first, not the revenue forecasts. Do not "plug" the revenue forecasts to fit anticipated spending. If adjusting expenses does not achieve acceptable financial outcomes, then all assumptions should be reviewed to see whether there are any adjustments that can be made in the basic framework of the program itself. For example, assumptions on class size, qualification level of staff, definition of market, and so forth may need to be challenged to see whether changes can result in a balanced budget while still meeting the basic mission of the project. This point in the planning creates a crucial "go/no-go" point. If the forecasts cannot support the financial viability of the initiative, it may need to be abandoned before any more resources are committed. If there is no margin, there is no mission, and failure on paper is preferable to the failure of a doomed start-up.

STEP 6: WRITING THE ACTION PLAN

At this point, all the gathered information can be pulled together into the action plan. The action plan should follow the basic outline presented at the beginning of this chapter. By following in order the previous five steps, the plan should have strong internal consistency and will provide a strong presentation while also serving as a valuable guide for the start-up process. The outline will present the information in an order that will flow more logically for the reader.

STEP 7: EXECUTIVE SUMMARY

The final step in developing the action plan is to write an executive summary. The executive summary serves as an overview of the entire plan that can communicate its essence within one or, at most, two pages. It is not simply an introduction to the action plan that grabs the readers' attention so that they read the whole plan. Instead, it should capture all the plan's main points and conclusions in a single page. The executive summary will serve as an important communication tool for the initiative with internal and external constituencies.

CONCLUSION

Part 1 of this book presented a model for the development of an entrepreneurial culture and management style for established school systems. The chapters in part 2 present specific tools and techniques that can be used within an entrepreneurial educational organization on a day-to-day basis.

REFERENCES

Allen, K. (1999). *Growing and managing an entrepreneurial business*. Boston: Houghton Mifflin.
Cornwall, J., and Perlman, B. (1990). *Organizational entrepreneurship*. Homewood, Ill.: Irwin.
Timmons, J. (1994). *New venture creation*. 4th ed. Boston: Irwin McGraw-Hill.

Part II

TOOLS AND TACTICS

7

MARKETING

There are two dimensions to marketing schools. One is to find out the thoughts of the public in the school's market area, and the other is to build a program to reach those people.

Determining public opinion concerning a school is considered a market research activity. In business, one definition of market research refers to activities conducted to establish the extent and location of the market; that is, the potential for sales of the products or services of the business. Market research can also be defined as the analysis of the costs and processes as compared with that of alternatives or competitors.

According to *Webster's Collegiate Dictionary* (10th edition), marketing is "the act or process of selling or purchasing in a market . . . an aggregate of functions involved in moving goods from producer to consumer."

The school is not in the businesses of selling a product, but it is providing a service. The marketing question is, then, how to get the school's service to the proper consumers. This usually means bringing the consumer (i.e., the student) to the school, although on occasion it is appropriate to bring the school services to the student.

At this point, it is appropriate to define *public relations* (which is covered in the next chapter) since it is one of the tools used in marketing. Public relations is the business of inducing the public to have a better understanding of and goodwill toward an institution. Another definition of the term is trying to bring about a harmony of understanding between an institution and the public it serves and on whose goodwill it depends.

For purposes of this discussion, the differentiation between public relations and marketing in education is as follows: Public relations deals with the communication between the school system and its publics about what *is;* marketing deals with the communication about what *might be*. Using this distinction, the same activities (e.g., press releases or opinion polls) may be used for either public relations or marketing purposes.

MARKETING THE SCHOOL

There is a saying in politics that there are two steps in getting elected to office. The first is to get known, and the second is to convince the public that you are the better or the best candidate. The same can be said about marketing an educational institution and its programs.

The first step in marketing the school is to make the public aware of the existence of the institution and its various programs. The next step is to convince the public of the quality of its programs to persuade potential students and their families that this would be the best institution for them. In many cases, the tools that are used to create public awareness can also be tools that are used for selling quality.

Before discussing techniques of marketing, it is necessary to examine strategies of successful marketing programs. First look at the institutional mission. The marketing program must be developed to be consistent with the belief statements, goals, and mission of the school. Only then it is appropriate to look at specific markets that the school intends to serve. Here are some things to consider:

1. *Examine the community's needs.* Are there new technical industries that need people trained for them? What are the expectations of area colleges and universities? What programs and values are expected by the community's employers?
2. *Identify underserved populations.* Are local schools neglecting populations from certain neighborhoods? Are people with disabilities, those with limited English-speaking ability, or other populations not being adequately served by existing schools?
3. *Determine the level of competition.* Is it desirable to take competitors on head-to-head? For example, if competitors offer an international baccalaureate program, would it be necessary to offer the same? Should counterprogramming be considered to offer alternatives to competitors?
4. *Try to define specific niches by developing new courses or programs, by refining existing programs, or by reinstituting ones that have been*

dropped. The market niche may be based on dramatic needs, but it may also be based on specific talents and skills of the school's employees as well as other resources of the school and community.

5. *Do not ignore population trends when examining markets.* It is important to know everything possible about population trends and issues. Is the number of births increasing or decreasing? Is there more in-migration or out-migration from primary service areas? Has there been any trend in the movement of students away from or toward the school or any of its competitors prior to the start of marketing efforts?

6. *Major concerns in developing a marketing program are the issues of transportation and communication.* How easy is it for students to get to and from the school? Are there population concentrations not being served that could be served by providing adequate transportation to the school or by bringing educational programs to the population centers? Is parking adequate if it is necessary for secondary students, and are there sufficient loading and unloading areas for parents transporting students to school?

7. *What is the nature of the communication systems used by the school? What are the plans for future development of the systems?* Would it be possible to teach students in remote locations by interactive television? What is the possibility of delivering some programs completely over the Internet to students in their homes, such as students who might otherwise be home schooling?

8. *Are facilities adequate?* If there is a successful marketing campaign, will facilities be adequate to accommodate the number of students who are attracted? Would it be necessary to consider offering some educational programs in remote and/or nontraditional locations? For example, could courses be offered in shopping centers, community centers, or even in churches in order to reach populations that might not otherwise participate in the school?

Addressing these issues will determine the general direction and emphasis of the marketing program.

Next, it is appropriate to determine the tools that will be used. Prior to that determination, it is a good idea to assemble stakeholders of the school to assess their perceptions of the strength and weaknesses in the marketplace. Successful marketing is based on potential users recognizing and responding to the strengths of the institution. What do potential students identify as the strengths of the school? List those strengths and rank them in priority order.

Next, look at perceived weaknesses. It does not matter whether the weakness actually exists or whether it is simply perceived as a weakness by potential users. In any case, it is necessary to reflect on what would appear to be the weaknesses of the school in the eyes of students, parents, and those who might be hiring graduates or admitting them to higher-education institutions. Of those perceived weaknesses, which appear to be the ones that are most important to the consumers?

After reviewing the perceived strengths and weaknesses, it is necessary to develop strategies that will convey the desired message based on the mission, goals, and programs of the school. There are many different ways to get the message out. The mechanics of dissemination tools is discussed in chapter 8. Here it is appropriate to suggest some specific activities that have been used by schools and other nonprofit organizations in marketing programs:

1. *Create a Web page for the Internet.*   While this is certainly a tool that is helpful in marketing to a local audience, it may be even more valuable if a school intends to extend its reach electronically. The use of Web pages is an example of how quickly technology can change the environment in which the school operates. Ten years ago, school Web pages were nonexistent, but now they are a necessity if the school is to be competitive in the market. The school may wish to work with an Internet provider such as Hifusion, which can help link the school Web page with current and potential students and their families.

2. *Make use of kiosks in shopping areas and other places where people congregate.*   Traditional kiosks that make available print materials or that run loop films have always been of some value, but computer-based kiosks create opportunities for people to learn about the school through an *interactive* program. Again, as with the Internet, these computer kiosks provide a modern way of marketing and demonstrate that the school understands and can use technology effectively.

3. *Use an educational "Welcome Wagon."*   An educational Welcome Wagon is a tool that has great potential for winning people over by providing a service that is useful and that shows the school's concern for someone new to the community. The Welcome Wagon technique requires access to lists of new residents. These lists can be obtained in a number of ways, such as by using the school census, public records of real estate transactions, or voter registration lists or by clipping stories from the local newspapers.

Once the lists are obtained, the school should develop a collection of welcoming materials that particularly relate to education and to community services available to residents. Examples of these materials are the school calendar and registration information, a listing of adult education programs available through school, school athletic events and concerts, and references to special help programs that are provided by the school itself or through commercial organizations such as the Sylvan Learning Centers or Kaplan.

Other useful information might include the location and hours of local libraries, the addresses and telephone numbers of higher-educational institutions within commuting distance, a list of scholarship opportunities available to people from the community or who attend your school, and information about public radio, public television, and public access television that would be providing programs of educational interest or concern. If there is great confidence in the quality of the school system, the list might even include competitor schools in the community to let the public know that there is awareness of other institutions but that there is no fear of competition.

If possible, this educational welcoming effort should include other non–school-related materials that are of value to residents, such as how and where to register to vote, where to apply for driver's licenses, where to get local property tax information, and how to contact public utilities.

The list that can be included in an educational Welcome Wagon type of offering is limited only by one's imagination. This service to new residents enables the school to establish relationships immediately and can be one of the best tools to promote its programs.

4. Establish advisory committees for both curricular and noncurricular concerns of the school. Some examples are an advisory group to explore additional fine arts opportunities for the community, an advisory committee to establish business education partnerships, or a task force on how to relate to changing demographic characteristics of the neighborhood and/or changing employment opportunities in the community. Each advisory committee creates opportunities for the school to reach out to people who might not otherwise have a natural relationship with the institution. This helps make people feel that they are a part of school—it no longer is your school but *our* school.

A word of caution: Advisory committees should not be used unless their advice is to be seriously considered. This does not mean that everything must be done as advisory committees recommend, but it does mean that the opinions of advisory committees and their members must be respected. It also means that it must be emphasized at every opportunity that advisory groups are not the final decision makers.

5. Establish a close working relationship with the chamber of commerce, commercial club, or other organization representing the business community. This can be started simply by joining the organization or by speaking at one of its meetings. Chapter 9 discusses the establishment of business education partnerships in detail.

6. Work with the real estate industry. It is a worthwhile investment of resources to spend time with real estate professionals to convince them of the quality of the school and to build a relationship so that they appreciate what the school has to offer. The most famous saying in real estate sales is that only three things matter: location, location, and location. One of the key elements relating to location is access to high-quality educational institutions.

A study was conducted in one urban community to determine what makes a stable community. Three factors were identified: a safe neighborhood, a clean neighborhood, and good schools. Good schools obviously are important to families with school-age children, but they can become a tool in marketing homes to others because they help maintain property values. Real estate professionals who are convinced that schools are high quality are very likely to distribute information about the schools in meetings with potential clients.

7. *Invite day care providers and parents to meet with the school's personnel.* This can be done by going to day care sites or by inviting people to the school, whichever is most convenient to them. Establishing a relationship with parents of preschool children will provide a competitive advantage at the time the students are ready to enroll in school. The school should not overlook its own or other schools' early childhood and family education programs when trying to build relationships with families of preschoolers.

8. *Seek cooperation from various retail businesses to make use of the free advertising they provide in some of their materials.* Paper liners for trays in fast-food restaurants and grocery bags at supermarkets frequently are made available to nonprofit organizations for publicity. This is too good an opportunity to pass up since it is a way to get the school's name before a large audience at no cost. Billboards and electronic signs might be used as well.

If the retailer is reluctant to have something that appears to be an ad for one school, this technique may be modified to promote a specific activity, such as a school volunteer program or American Education Week, which still puts the name, address, and phone number of the school before the public.

9. *Make sure that there are print materials and possibly audiovisual materials available in languages other than English.* Have these available for groups that are represented in substantial numbers in the community and for groups that are small but appear to be growing. Even if the students themselves have English as their primary language, parents and grandparents may still speak another language in the home.

Having materials printed in the languages that these adults can understand is a sign of respect for them and an opportunity to bring parents and grandparents as well as children into a partnership with the school.

10. *Provide school–community service projects.* Students working on environmental cleanup, providing services to shut-ins, and providing child care for mothers in parent education programs are examples of these kinds of projects. A service learning program can greatly enhance the school's image through the service activities.

11. Serve as a polling place for local elections. It is generally recognized that people are more likely to have a positive attitude about the school if they have set foot in the building for any reason during the year. Many people form their opinions about local schools on the basis of the most negative things they see and hear in the national news media.

Offering the schools as a polling place for local elections creates an opportunity for many people who are not associated with the schools to come into the building and see it as it really is. Careful attention should be given to the displays in the school at the time of elections, and material should be available near the polling place for people interested in information about the school.

In states where it is legal, the school can combine service activities with election activities by offering rides to the polls for people who do not have transportation of their own.

12. Provide an informal intake planning session with students and parents. While not as formal as the joint school–parent planning that goes into an Individualized Education Plan for special education, the local administrator and teacher might sit down with the prospective student and parents to go over the interests of the family, common concerns about the education of the child, and the opportunities in the school.

This approach focuses on educational needs of the student, but it also sets a positive tone for school–family relationships from the beginning. This is especially important for parents who have had negative experiences of their own because of either academic problems or disciplinary issues when they were in school.

MARKET RESEARCH

Market research in education means using techniques and activities of systematically collecting, analyzing, and interpreting information that can assist educators in determining the best ways to market their programs.

Market research in education deals with matters such as acquiring data on existing markets using qualitative and quantitative techniques to increase enrollment in the school, determining the needs of the customers (students, parents, and taxpayers), determining the market share of competitors, testing programs in the marketplace to determine their effectiveness, estimating enrollment, and ultimately developing maximum enrollment for the school system.

Market research can be a very sophisticated and complex subject worthy of a college major. This chapter deals only with practical techniques that can be used by practicing school administrators. There should be no need to spend money on experts. People within the school—be they administrators, teachers, students, or volunteers—can do everything suggested here.

Here are the five elements of basic market research for schools:

1. *Collecting basic factual information about the school and community.* In order to understand one's place in the market, it is important to gather as much useful information as possible. School records, such as the school census, enrollment figures, dropout rate, and transfer rate, are important in assessing market position. The U.S. Census Bureau has a substantial amount of information available not only on the total population but also broken down by age, racial group, income level, nature of household, percentage of the households with telephones, and so forth. All this information is of value to the person who assesses the place of the school in the market.

Other sources of information can be very useful. For example, municipal officials keep track of housing starts or building permits granted. This provides an opportunity to determine the potential growth in the community. The amount of information collected by state agencies and the size and sophistication of the government structures where the school is located all have a bearing on how much of this useful demographic data are available.

As people in the school become more sophisticated at collecting and utilizing data, it should be possible to find additional sources that will expand the ability to use this information in a constructive way for the benefit of the school.

2. *Collecting information through surveys of entire populations.* The advantage of taking an entire group of people and surveying them as opposed to sampling is that there is less argument about the validity of the survey and the ability of the school to get accurate information. For example, a useful marketing tool is the regular follow-up study of the school's graduates. Establishing follow-up studies at regular intervals, such as one and five years after graduation, may yield a substantial amount of useful information. The first follow-up gives the students' immediate impressions of the value of their school experience as they enter higher education or the labor market. The second follow-up enables the students who have completed their preemployment education or who have worked for several years to put their education into a proper context.

These surveys provide an opportunity to determine the relevance of the programs to the recent graduates. The surveys also give an assessment of the quality of the school programs in the views of an important audience: the alumni.

It is often more important to survey the people who have dropped out. What is the reason for the dropout? It may be financial, a move to another location, personality conflicts, a feeling of lack of success, a job opportunity, or many other things. The school is not going to know unless the students who dropped out are asked. This type of survey is best done individually in a person-to-person interview so that there is an opportunity to follow up on initial questions and to look for secondary or hidden reasons other than the stated ones obtained from a paper-and-pencil survey.

While all attempts to survey an entire population can yield valuable information, the surveys that get the highest percentage response obviously are of the greatest value. Getting substantial response is relatively easy for the students who are currently enrolled in the program. It is somewhat more difficult with graduates or dropouts after they have left the system for any lengthy period of time.

One value of collecting this kind of data is that, if done on a regular basis, it is possible to assess longitudinal trends. These provide clues relating to perceived changes in attitudes about the quality and content of the educational program.

3. Ongoing data collection in conjunction with the school's regular day-to-day activities.   This is a relatively easy way to get much useful information. Staff should be given notice as to what kinds of information should be kept and how that information should be recorded. For example, at a parent conference day, it would be good for each teacher to make a brief summary of the kinds of comments parents have made about the school, in particular any problems or issues that the students have.

Telephone logs of incoming calls should be kept for the principal's office (and classrooms where phones are available). At a minimum, these logs would be kept only to determine the nature of the call (was it a question, complaint, suggestion, or request?). It is useful to keep a record of calls that are complimentary about the school, staff, students, or programs. Of equal value, however, are calls that may have specific complaints. Knowing the concerns of people who are motivated enough to call can be very useful in dealing with the marketing of the school. Of course, there are certain individuals who may make crank calls and distort the impressions of the school unless it is noted who the source of the complaints is.

Another informal technique to collect information on an ongoing basis is informal surveys. These do not attempt to be scientific in their sampling, nor are they distributed to an entire population; rather, they are simply made available at school events, such as parent conferences, concerts, plays, science fairs, and other activities that would bring large numbers of people into the building. Using schools as polling places for general elections creates an opportunity to put out surveys to get the general public's impressions of the school.

This kind of survey does not attempt a sophisticated analysis of the percentage of people who feel one way or another, but it is simply an attempt to determine the kinds of concerns on people's minds and possibly the intensity of those concerns.

There are many other ongoing activities that can be done to help establish a database of opinion that would be useful for the school. For example, someone can clip articles (and especially letters to the editor) from local news media to assess attitudes toward the school or get the same kind of information from student newspapers. In this way, it is possible to take a long-term look at the success of the school in getting fair and accurate information to the public.

4. Focus groups.　The term *focus group* has been used in market research in a variety of ways. Focus groups are used to evaluate programs already in existence, to develop surveys that might ask questions of a wider audience, to get the participants to interpret earlier information that they may have received, or to seek information about potential new programs needed or wanted.

Some groups attempt to schedule focus groups in which all the participants are alike. For example, everyone in the focus group lives in a certain community, all are parents of students in band, or all are senior citizens or members of some other identifiable group.

Others like to use focus groups to elicit information from cross sections of people. Therefore, when deciding whether to use a focus group, you first need to determine the purpose of the focus group and thereby the members making up that group.

Planning for focus groups has to include a determination of the number of groups, the size of the groups, the source of the participants, and the level of involvement of the moderator or facilitator.

It must be emphasized that focus groups are not a way to get an accurate reflection of the opinion of the average person in the district; rather, they are a way to generate ideas and get creative responses to existing ideas or programs.

Some people, for convenience purposes, take a ready-made group to serve as a focus group. This could be people on a parent advisory committee who would be asked to serve as a focus group for a potential new program. A group of students who have been subject to a disciplinary policy may be asked to be a focus group to respond to that specific policy. Student government or a committee thereof could be a focus group for specific activities.

To get the best information and to give maximum benefit to the school from the use of a focus group, the group should represent a relatively broad cross section of people. Several focus groups could be conducted, each of which could be fairly narrow in composition as long as individual groups are taken from different constituencies or populations in the school.

The focus group can be defined as a setting in which eight to twelve respondents discuss a given topic in the presence of a well-trained, objective facilitator. The focus group has the advantage of being versatile and providing a lot of data that could not be elicited from a formal, written survey. Another clear advantage is that it can be used by people who are unsure of their ability to apply formal statistical research. On the other hand, it should be noted that focus groups cannot be used to generalize results.

The disadvantage of focus groups is that they are only as effective as the ability of the facilitator to keep the group on the subject and stimulate discussion from members of the group without dominating or directing the participants in a specific direction.

As for conducting focus groups for the school, an experienced school administrator, possibly a social studies teacher or any teacher who leads discussions that evoke responses from students, could handle this task with a minimum of training. The task of the facilitator is to get the general subject before the participants and to encourage them and bring them out to discuss the issue at hand in a free and open manner.

The focus group session probably should not last more than an hour and a half. The session should be recorded, or, at a minimum, the facilitator or a recorder should take notes. The facilitator might open the session with a discussion of what the topic is to be. The facilitator should have in mind two or three subtopics that can be raised to stimulate the discussion, if necessary.

Focus groups give people an opportunity to make specific comments, to express strong feelings, and to put things in very personal terms that might not be possible in a closed-response survey. The name implies that focus groups should not deal with diverse subjects. For consistency, if more than one focus group is to be held and if there are different moderators, the moderators should be given a specific list of questions or topics to be covered and possibly even a script for the opening statement. Once the focus groups are finished, data should be assembled and reported as soon as possible.

Focus groups are helpful in understanding the needs, attitudes, and perspectives of the customers of the school. They can be very helpful in determining programs that might be offered and in getting reactions to proposed brochures, recruiting letters, television programs, or other techniques that might be used to explain the school's activities or initiatives.

5. *Statistical sampling.* Scientific sampling of public opinion is used to determine the attitudes of an entire population without spending the time and the money necessary to seek the opinions of everyone in that population. Successful sampling of public opinion accurately reflects the views of the population, minimizes statistical error, maximizes convenience, and minimizes cost.

Opinion sampling is relatively easy to do and does not require the substantial expense of retaining consultants. With the basic techniques suggested here, a group of willing volunteers with minimal training can conduct a survey that is adequate for the vast majority of purposes. This does not mean that results of a referendum can be predicted within 1 or 2 percent of the actual vote, as is done by sophisticated pollsters for politicians and major news media.

When polling for marketing purposes, all that is necessary is to get a general interest. For example, if sentiment for adding Japanese to the Modern Language program is being tested, it does not make much difference whether the percentage of people interested in a new program is 52 or 41 percent since either one would be more than adequate to justify the existence of a new program.

When determining sample size, two serious issues arise. The first is the definition of a *statistically* adequate size, and the second is the definition of a *politically* adequate sample size. From a purely statistical standpoint, a sample of size 30, if correctly drawn, may be adequate to indicate the general views of a population of any size. Politically, a sample that small would be difficult to explain to a population that does not understand sampling statistics if the sample is drawn from a group as large as all voters in a large school district.

One way of estimating the accuracy of a sample size that is adequate for purposes of educational market research is to divide 1 by the square root of the number in the sample. The resulting answer is the percentage of error that would be likely to occur in that situation. For example, if the sample size were 100, 1 over the square root of 100 is 1 over 10, or 10 percent sampling error. If the sample size were 400, 1 over the square root of 400 equals 1 over 20, or 5 percent sampling error. If the sample size were 1,600, the calculation would yield 1 over 40, or 2.5 percent sampling error.

Taking the example of a sample size of 400, the likely error would be about 5 percent, so if the result came out that 60 percent of the sample favored a proposal, the odds are that the real percentage would be within 5 percent one way or another of that figure, or between 55 and 65 percent. As one can see, this is not perfectly accurate, but it is very reasonable since the results of attitude surveys are going to change from day to day, depending on a variety of factors. In making marketing decisions, the general trend is the important thing.

As this short statistical exercise shows, greater accuracy results from increasing the size of the sample, but a point of diminishing returns comes quickly once the sample size gets over 1,000. In most cases, surveys for news media and politicians tend to feel that a sample size anywhere from 400 to 1,500 is more than adequate for surveying statewide or even nationwide populations. Obviously, if that is adequate for those large populations, samples of this magnitude should be more than adequate for a school district or attendance area.

Statistics mentioned here are based on simple random sampling, which is like putting all the names of the people in the population to be sampled in a hat and then pulling out the number of names needed for the sample at random. One technique that can increase the accuracy of sampling is *stratified random sampling,* in which a proportionate number of names are drawn from different geographic areas or other strata that would accurately reflect your school district. For example, in assessing attitudes about education in three adjacent communities, one of which had 20 percent of the population, another 35 percent of the population, and another 45 percent of the population, the sample could be drawn proportionately from each of the communities.

Random sampling requires that each unit have an *equal* chance of being selected for the sample and that each unit have an *independent* chance of being selected for the sample. That is why it is suggested that the names be literally pulled out of a hat for a small population or be identified some other way (such as assigning computer-generated random numbers to each individual) so that the sample can be drawn without any statistical bias.

Pure random sampling is difficult to do with large populations, where it is unclear who is in the population. The first question is to determine what is the population (sometimes called the "universe") to be sampled. The population could be all adults in a school district, all households in a district, all registered voters, or all parents of children in the school system. When drawing the sample, it is important to know what the population is, as the results can be generalized only to that population and not to others. If the sample is drawn only from parents of one school, the results cannot be used to generalize about the attitudes of nonparents who live in the community or of those who are parents of students in another school.

Systematic selection is a technique for drawing a sample quickly. Technically, it is not as accurate as random sampling, but for practical purposes it can be used in the kinds of surveys that schools do. With systematic selection, once the population is determined, the population is divided by the number that is to be in a sample. The result is the sampling interval. This can be expressed by the simple formula $P/N = I$, where P is the size of the total population, N is the size of the sample, and I is the sampling interval. One must randomly select the first unit of the sample from the first interval. After the first unit is chosen completely at random, then every Ith unit of the population is selected for the sample. This means that each unit has an equal (but not an independent) chance of being selected.

Statistical precision is of not great importance to the practical school leader who is trying to find general information. The bottom line is that systematic selection allows a simple technique for quickly drawing a sample.

Consider a situation in which the entire population to be surveyed consists of registered voters in the community. If there were 6,000 registered voters and a sample of 400 were desired, the sampling interval would be 15 (6,000/400 = 15). You take the registered voters list and, of the first 15 names, put those numbers in a hat and draw one out. If the number drawn were 7, then name number 7 would go in the sample. You add the sampling interval (15) to the number drawn (7) to get the next name (22). You keep adding the sampling interval (15) to get succeeding members of the sample, such as numbers 37, 52, 67, and so forth, until the entire sample of 400 names is drawn.

Consider another example. You draw a sample of 50 parents from a school with a population of 1,000 parents. In order to get a quick survey, you divide 1,000 (P) by 50 (N) and get a sampling interval (I) of 20. From the list of parents, a simple draw of random numbers between 1 and 20 will provide the first person to be in the sample. For example, if you draw number 14, the 14th name on the list will be in the sample. The sampling interval (20) is added to 14 to get 34, the number of the second person in the sample. You continue with each 20th name until the sample is complete.

It is obvious from this discussion that there must be a database from which a sample can be drawn. In some cases, the database is not completely accurate for the population desired. For example, to sample all households in the community, the only reasonable database that may be readily available is the telephone book. If a sample is drawn from the telephone book, by either random sampling or systematic selection, an additional type of error is added to the study in that not all households have telephones and some people have unlisted numbers. These are some of the issues to be considered in determining the accuracy and appropriateness of the chosen population even before deciding the sampling method.

While the sampling method is very important, of equal importance is the ability to write unbiased questions for the interviews. Questions used should be fair, understandable, and of value to the school. One does not do a service to an institution by stacking the deck and asking questions that will distort the real opinions of the population. These questions may be good for political propaganda purposes, but they are ethically suspect and of no value in terms of market research.

Priorities must be established in deciding what questions should be in a survey. A common mistake is to ask too many questions, including some for which the answers are of no value at all in relation to the purpose of the survey. Any survey that is to be used should be field tested to see that the questions are understandable, are perceived as being fair by an unbiased respondent, and are not so numerous as to cause the respondents to lose interest.

The number and complexity of the questions that are asked will vary, depending on the technique used for polling. It is possible to ask many more questions and questions that build on one another in a face-to-face interview than it would be in a telephone interview. The least satisfactory method of sampling opinion is by mail, although that is the only practical method in many circumstances.

GENERAL ISSUES IN DATA COLLECTION

In most methods of data collection, including sampling statistics, surveys of general populations, and focus groups, there are several things that need to be remembered:

1. *The time period for data collection should not be too long.* If the data gathering takes too long, there can be several negative or compounding factors. The responses may be impacted by major news events. It will be more difficult to maintain the morale of volunteers who are collecting the data. If the data collection period is very long, there is even the risk of loss of interest on the part of the people who are expected to use the data. Most important, if the interval of collecting information is too long, some of the data may become dated or even useless before the research is finished.

Some suggested time limits for data collection include one week for telephone surveys, two weeks for face-to-face interviews, and four weeks for mail surveys (including the time for the follow-up to the original mailing).

2. *Cover letters are very important in establishing credibility in doing opinion sampling.* It is becoming more difficult to establish credibility for a valid market survey. This is because so many business groups are doing marketing surveys, so many politicians are doing opinion sampling, and so many salespeople are claiming to do a survey when they are really in the business of direct sales.

One way to establish that credibility is through the use of a cover letter. A cover letter can explain who is doing the survey, the importance of the survey, and the assurance of respondent anonymity. The cover letter can offer a way to get questions answered by those people who are interested in knowing more about the survey.

In mail surveys, the cover letter can accompany the survey. The cover letter for in-person interviews should be sent at least one week before the interview is to take place. For telephone interviews, the traditional pattern once was not to send a cover letter unless there was unusual resistance to the interview. Now, because of the enormous number of sales and other personnel using what appears to be telephone market survey techniques, it would be wise to send a cover letter ahead of any telephone survey.

One recent study showed almost a 50 percent refusal rate for people called in telephone surveys. It cannot be assumed that those who refuse to respond have similar opinions to those who do participate, so it is important to keep the refusal rate as low as possible. Some political pollsters suggest that they must make ten or more calls to complete one.

3. *Many marketing businesses offer some kind of incentive for participating in a survey.* These incentives could be cash, gift certificates, or other kinds of tangible benefits. There are problems in the schools trying to use these kinds of incentives. It may appear to some that school money is being spent on something that is not appropriately a school activity, although tickets to a school play or concert may be considered a reasonable incentive to be provided by the school system if an incentive is needed. This is the kind of issue that should be discussed within the community before a final decision is made.

For most data collection techniques, it is important to see that there is adequate preparation and supervision of the people who will be gathering information. The interviewers, the survey developers and analysts, and the moderators for focus groups should have appropriate training and written instructions or checklists, and they should be conducting their processes in a standardized way.

Supervisors should monitor these processes and provide encouragement for the people doing the actual surveying and help when it is needed. It is important for the supervisors to see that follow-up is done in personal interviews and telephone surveys. With telephone surveys, it is important (if possible) to have all the phoning done from a single location so that adequate supervision and support can be provided. No unsupervised phoning from home should be done because this invariably leads to either not getting the job done or people saying it was done when it really was not. Chapter 11 has more detailed suggestions in setting up telephone banks.

SUGGESTED ACTIVITIES

1. Gather demographic data from multiple sources (the census, local and state planning agencies, and the state education agency) and study trends that might affect school population.
2. Collect information about the competition: recruiting materials, new programs, and enrollment trends.
3. Meet with business leaders to get their perceptions of education needs in the community.
4. Identify businesses that might help publicize the school and its programs.
5. Identify staff, students, or friends of the school who could do opinion

sampling. One possibility might be an interdisciplinary project between a social studies class (developing the content) and a math class or a marketing class (developing the mechanics of polling).

6. Survey the community about the perceived strengths and weaknesses of the school.
7. Conduct a training session for focus group facilitators to prepare them for working with a group.
8. Create marketing materials that can be displayed when the school is hosting public events, such as concerts, plays, open houses, community meetings, and elections.
9. Do a community education needs assessment to help determine school offerings for adults and non–school-age children.

RESOURCES

Lusch, Robert F., and Lusch, Virginia N. (1987). *Principles of marketing.* Boston: Kent Publishing.

National PTA. (2000). *Building successful partnerships: A guide to developing parent and family involvement programs.* Bloomington, Ind.: National Education Services.

Zigmund, William G. (1986). *Exploring marketing research.* 2nd ed. Chicago: Dryden Press.

8

TELLING YOUR STORY:
PERCEPTION *IS* REALITY

This chapter deals with the ability of a school to communicate effectively with its many and varied publics. The ability to communicate frequently means the difference between success and failure in educational leadership.

PURPOSES OF PUBLIC SCHOOL RELATIONS

The American Association of School Administrators (1950, 14) listed the following purposes for school public relations:

- Inform the public about the work of the school
- Establish confidence in the school
- Rally support for the maintenance of the educational program
- Develop awareness of the importance of education in a democracy
- Improve partnership concept by uniting parents and teachers in meeting the educational needs of students
- Integrate the home, school, and community in improving educational opportunities for all learners
- Evaluate the offerings of the school in meeting the needs of the learners in the community
- Correct misunderstandings as to the aims and objectives of the school

As can be seen in this list, the basic purposes of public relations have not changed in over fifty years. While effective school leaders always knew and used public relations tools, in recent years there has been a greater emphasis on the importance of public relations.

PRINCIPLES OF PUBLIC RELATIONS

Effective public relations is based on several important principles. These principles must be adhered to if one is going to have a credible institution in education as in any other field.

First, public relations must be based on reality. There is a saying in the public relations field that "You don't sell the steak, you sell the sizzle." The problem is that one cannot sell the sizzle if there "ain't no steak." Public relations programs fall flat when there is an attempt to make a situation look better than it really is.

A related principle is that there must be honesty in what is said and done. An example of what *not* to do was the school system that put all the students from several lunch shifts in the cafeteria at the same time for a picture to be used in promoting a bond issue to relieve overcrowding in the school. People with knowledge of the school realized that there were multiple lunch shifts, so grouping the students together at the same time in the lunchroom clearly was deceptive advertising. Credibility lost by this kind of activity is very difficult, if not impossible, to regain.

Public relations activities of the school should be positive. This does not mean ignoring the negative activities, but it does mean, as the old song says, "accentuate the positive." In working with students, it is common to take their strengths and build on them. In like manner, the strengths of the school should be emphasized in building a public relations program.

There will be situations in which individuals or groups will try to portray the school in a bad light. Responding to an allegation often gives more credibility to the charge. Attempts to make denials of allegations that are clearly false or misleading should be made only if the school seems to be hurt by the publicity. Dealing with these situations requires planning and preparation on the part of the school in determining when and how it may be appropriate to respond to attacks.

Another obvious principle is that the public relations activity must be ongoing. Some schools appear to be interested in their publics only before a bond election or a levy referendum. Others seem to be interested in relating to the public only when they have a very successful athletic team or when they are try-

ing to disprove some allegation made about the quality of the school or the behavior of the students. The ongoing program will not have the problems of
those programs that merely react to specific incidents.

The program must be balanced and comprehensive, relating to all aspects of
the school at all times of the school year and vacation periods. It must use all
possible communications resources. School administrators sometimes get so
obsessed with a unique or cute tool of public relations that they forget the necessity of a comprehensive program.

The program must deal with all publics. At a time in which approximately 80
percent of the households in the nation do not have children in school, it would
be folly to think that an effective public relations program is one that deals with
parents only. Taxpayer groups, senior citizens, singles, and those who might
have children in other types of schools are all appropriate publics for the school
system. Not to be forgotten are the school's internal publics, including teachers, other staff, administrators, and, most important, the students.

The changing demographics of society require that the school system review
its public relations programs frequently in order to effectively deal with new
populations that may not have existed in the community before. In St. Paul,
Minnesota, for example, the movement of the Hmong community to the
United States as a result of the Vietnam War has created a population that has
become the largest single minority group in the school system in a relatively
short period of time.

Even small towns and rural areas that historically have been homogeneous in
terms of race, religion, and nationality are finding that, with the mobility of the
population, changing birth rates, and immigration, the nature of their communities is changing. What once were farming communities may now find that
telecommuting and decentralization of manufacturing are bringing people with
different skills and backgrounds to the community.

Public relations is a two-way communication. Schools must do a better job of
seeking out the ideas of the many and varied publics they serve. If one looks at
public relations as selling, then it is instructive to look at the techniques of good
salespersons. Those who are the most successful in the sales fields are not the
ones who talk the most but the ones who listen the most. By listening, one can
identify the concerns of others so that those concerns can be met. Also, by listening, an individual is showing respect for those to whom they listen. Unfortunately, schools are not always seen as having respect for the opinions and
ideas of many of their publics.

Another very important principle of public relations is the so-called KISS
concept: Keep It Simple, Stupid. Educators frequently fall into the trap of using
professional jargon and acronyms that are not known to the general public.

When preparing a written or oral presentation, it always helps to have the statement reviewed by someone not connected to the school to see that no language is included that is incomprehensible to outsiders. Professional language does have its place in providing a shorthand method of communication between those who understand the language, but it can appear arrogant and off-putting in interactions with people who are not a part of the profession's in-group.

The final principle that must be remembered is that *there are no panaceas.* There are no magic bullets. There are no situations where one can say, "If only we did this one thing, we would have perfect public relations." As with virtually every other endeavor, there is no simple solution that will solve all problems. One must take all these principles and develop practical methods of implementing them in order to have an effective public relations program.

TEN TIPS FOR OPERATING A PUBLIC RELATIONS PROGRAM

1. *Be prepared.* Preparation means analyzing all the elements that are necessary for the success of a program: who does it, how the program is connected, the tools that need to be used for the success of a program, outlooks for communication, and the nature of the publics.
2. *Be organized.* Preparation lays the groundwork, and organization enables the program to function. In every situation, determine who is in charge, what the time table is, and what activities are to take place. Only with these basic elements of organization in place will there be an opportunity to conduct a successful program.
3. *Be informed.* Adequate knowledge of the subject, the people involved, and the processes is necessary if the program is to be effective.
4. *Be available.* Unfortunately, school leaders frequently seem to disappear when it comes to certain public relations activities, such as meeting with the news media or responding to a crisis. Availability frequently is a most important asset in relating to the news media.
5. *Be prompt.* In responding to a request or in dealing with a major issue, it is important to be prompt. When one does not respond in a timely fashion to a crisis, a question, or an issue, it may appear that the school is hiding something or that a response may not be what people want to hear. A classic example of this kind of public relations crisis happened to the British royal family on the death of Princess Diana. Because the family took several days before they made any public announcements and displays of their feelings, their credibility was dramatically undermined with the population. It took weeks to even partially undo the damage.

6. *Be open.* It is not enough to be available; one also has to be open and above board. This does not mean baring one's soul or giving away the family secrets, but it does mean being forthright and direct in responding to inquiries. Sometimes it may be necessary to say, "I don't know" or "I'll have to find more information" or "I'll get back to you." Usually, the worst thing to say is, "No comment," but unfortunately this is what many school leaders say as a result of having watched too much television.

7. *Be accurate.* It is important not to make statements when one is not sure of the facts. A lack of accuracy can lead to a lack of credibility. Realistically, everyone makes mistakes occasionally, and when that is done, it should be acknowledged immediately and efforts at accuracy redoubled.

8. *Be friendly.* The public and the news media are not the enemy. If one sees them as the enemy, it usually invokes a reciprocal negative response. It should be obvious that it is easier to build relationships with people when one is friendly than when one is not.

   Too often school officials do not interact with the media until there is a crisis. Smart educators will invite media people to school or go to their offices with no agenda other than to get acquainted.

9. *Be positive.* This means not only being positive about the accomplishments and activities of the school and its personnel but also being positive in the relationships with people inside and outside of the school. There is a tendency to be negative toward people who are perceived as critics when in many cases they may be doing you a favor by publicly raising concerns that others may have. A negative attitude to these critics will only further alienate them and others who do not speak up.

10. *Be creative.* In attempting to build relationships with one's publics, it is important to try new means of communication. Competition for the attention of the public is intense. The only way to get people's attention may be by doing something new or unique. Also, the best way to get communication *from* the public may be some new or innovative method that has not been used before.

WHO TELLS THE SCHOOL'S STORY?

The simple answer to this question is everyone connected with the institution. Each person connected with the school can have an impact on the attitude of the public. Anecdotal reports abound about the impact that one disgruntled secretary or janitor can have in talking to their friends and neighbors about what went on at the school. Salespersons traveling from school to school are great carriers of information or, on some occasions, misinformation.

As a school develops its public relations program, thought must be given to how everyone connected with the institution gets information. This includes teachers, other staff, students, parents, school board, and members of the community at large.

Responsibility for developing the public relations program is with the administrators. However, they may delegate much of the detail of operating the program to others. For example, parents or other community people who are professionals in the field of public relations or advertising may be willing to do pro bono work as volunteers in helping tell the story of the school. Some teachers, particularly in the area of communications, may have skills to contribute as a volunteer or maybe can have some public relations functions made a part of their job assignment. Classes in journalism, art, graphic design, or computer technology may be instrumental in helping develop effective communication methods for the school.

It is necessary to conduct an inventory of the talents, abilities, and interests of people connected with the school in determining who should be involved in the official public relations program. This means identifying interests and abilities of students, teachers, parents, and community members and then using approaches from the volunteer program, from staff assignment, and from experiential learning activities of students to organize the personnel in a way that is most effective for the school.

Plans must be made to see that all members of the school community understand their role in telling the school's story and have made available to them the information necessary to be informed so that their conversations about the school and their activities relating to the school are accurate.

A word of caution about using students. They may be used to help *tell* about the school, but they should not be used to *sell* the school. For example, if it appears that school officials are manipulating students to promote a referendum, there could be a disastrous blow to the school's credibility.

REACHING OUT TO THE COMMUNITY

Schools frequently fall into the trap of talking to people but not listening to them. A variety of tools and techniques should be used to make sure that there is an adequate opportunity to get communication to the school. Several of those are discussed here.

The use of *advisory groups* is one technique to get opinions from the public. Some advisory groups are permanent, and others are short term, serving a specific purpose. Whenever advisory groups are employed, it is imperative to get them to understand that they are advisory only. Often, members of advisory groups are disappointed and angry if their recommendations are not taken in total. Advisory group members must be told their role when they are asked to serve and reminded of it at virtually every meeting. It should also be made clear who is responsible for final decisions.

In the selection of advisory groups, it is important to see that various individuals, groups, and points of view are represented. One way to do this is to open membership to all volunteers. Another way is to use what is sometimes known as the "Noah's Ark" approach: making a best effort to select individuals or groups from each identifiable organization or interest group in the community. Even if the school selects the advisory committee, it may be good politics to allow anyone who strongly requests an opportunity to serve to do so. A basic approach to dealing with agitators and critics is to bring them into the decision-making process so that they become a part of the system rather than merely outsiders who can criticize without any sense of responsibility.

Other methods of reaching out include the marketing techniques discussed in the previous chapter, including *surveys* and *focus groups*. While it may not be feasible to do a scientific survey each time you are seeking information from the public, it is easy to use informal surveys at meetings or to put a survey in the newspaper or a newsletter to get a general sense of opinion, realizing that this is not a scientific representation of the entire community. In the same vein, focus groups can help identify or define issues or potential solutions to problems, but the focus group is not an attempt to get a detailed cross section of public opinion.

Open houses or other activities that bring large groups of people into the school are another opportunity to reach out. Casual conversations with people at open houses, parents' nights, science fairs, athletic events, or any other activity that draws people to the school can provide useful information. It is also possible to do brief surveys of people as they come to the school for these kinds of events.

The concept of *listening hours* is one that has been used effectively to reach out to the community. In some cases, school administrators or other designated listeners for the school have regular office hours in which people can come in and visit them. While this is beneficial, it severely limits who can take advantage of this opportunity.

For example, an inner-city school principal dealing with sensitive race relations problems thought that he was doing the right thing by having two hours of an open-door policy once a week in his office for any citizen to come in and talk to him. In his neighborhood, many low-income citizens did not have transportation to get to the school, and many of the others, who worked during school hours, could come only if they took off work. The intention of the principal was laudable, but the method left a lot to be desired.

A better method used by some school leaders is to go into the community and meet with people on their own turf. This eliminates the transportation problem for some people. If the educational leader goes out at various times during the day, it also eliminates the problem of the community member who cannot get in during the normal school day. The location may make a big difference in the level of participation.

One suburban superintendent was successful by sitting at a table in the lobby of the bank on Friday evenings (payday for many people), available for anyone who wanted to come and see him. Others have found that holding listening sessions in the larger grocery stores is very useful since every family must eat.

In some communities, the school can identify specific institutions where the people feel comfortable and may be much more likely to discuss their concerns. For example, in many African-American neighborhoods, the church is often the center of community activity. While some public school administrators are squeamish about church–state relationships, reality dictates that if the church is where people gather and feel comfortable, then that is the place to meet them.

With senior citizens, who are frequently seen as opponents of school funding because of their concern about property taxes, it might be a neighborhood center. School leaders who go to senior citizens' centers have an opportunity to build relationships and find out the specific concerns of older citizens.

Public forums are another opportunity to reach out. The school can sponsor forums in which people from a variety of perspectives and organizations can have an opportunity to participate. For example, some people are concerned about the morning start time of schools and its impact on the health of teenagers. A school could sponsor a forum that would bring together health care providers, police officers, employers of student part-time workers, school personnel, parents, and students. By sponsoring the forum, the school demonstrates an interest in reaching out to the public and at the same time gathers useful data in order to make a more informed decision.

School personnel can also participate in public forums sponsored by others; in doing so, they have an opportunity to interact with different elements of the community. With the integration of public services becoming a matter of concern, it would be useful for the schools to cooperate with health, law enforcement, social welfare, and other community agencies in sponsoring public forums that would relate to matters of interest to all those elements of the community. The act of partnering with other organizations builds relationships with them, and the results of the activities can enable schools to develop alternative ways of dealing with matters of concern to all interested parties.

Presentations made by members of the school to community organizations (whether it be an athletic boosters club, a business persons association, a church organization, a veterans club, or any other kind of community group) will give the sensitive school leader the opportunity to speak, to listen to formal discussion following the presentation, and to participate in informal conversation before and after the event. These events provide more insights as to the thinking of the general public and can be beneficial simply by allowing people to "blow off steam."

Newer means of reaching out include *electronic dialogues* through the Internet or voice mail. This is particularly helpful because it allows people to interact at their own convenience. Technology may also enable people to give their honest opinions from home in relative anonymity, so there is less concern about the political correctness of the comments. The downside of this technology is that there may be people making outrageous remarks, saying things that are not true, or are using language that is inappropriate.

TOOLS OF COMMUNICATION

Broadcast Television

The opportunities in broadcast television will vary with the size of the community and the availability of local broadcast television stations. In large communities, it is difficult for an individual school to get airtime on a broadcast television station. In very small towns, there are no television stations. In communities with populations of 25,000 to 100,000 that have television stations, the opportunity for the school to get some time is better. The reality is that the opportunity for airtime is limited in almost all communities, but creative schools can find ways to get something on a local broadcast station.

The school must build a relationship with the television station. One way to get station representatives into your school is to invite them to speak to an entire assembly of the student body or to have career days during which television reporters or others connected with the business are invited to speak. This gives school officials an opportunity to build personal relationships with some of the employees of the station. If schools have communications classes, it may be possible to take field trips to the station, giving the station staff a chance to interact with individual students and teachers.

Inviting news teams to cover what the school sees as newsworthy events is one of the ways in which you build a relationship. It must be remembered that the media will not respond to all invitations. There may be too much breaking news, or the station may be shorthanded or feel that the school event is not of interest to a wide enough audience. Media-wise educators know that if they issue enough invitations, there will eventually be some positive responses.

Another approach is to provide background briefings on matters that might not be of immediate news interest but that might be useful for the station to know for future reference.

Many television stations run news features about people in the community, for example, the athlete of the week among the high school athletes in the area served by the station. While this may not present a balanced view of the school, it is helpful for the school to get this kind of exposure, and it is an opportunity for educators to talk to station personnel about other possible features, such as outstanding students in academic competitions, unusual activities of school personnel, or recognition earned by teachers in the school.

Nonathletic competitions (e.g., science fairs, math counts, Olympiads of the mind, high school bowls, and so forth) have been used effectively by schools to focus on students in a positive way. The renewed popularity of quiz shows on television and the Internet may make local stations more interested in academic competitions. While some schools downplay competition, the reality is that the public is drawn to the outstanding student who succeeds in a competition, whether it be in athletics, fine arts, academics, or any other arena.

Schools can generate activities that have value as news features. Two examples are sponsoring a music or art festival (which shows that the school is a cultural center for the whole community) and having the students do curricular-related activities to preserve the environment (which demonstrates that the school is a responsible community member).

Schools may have some opportunity to get exposure on television through general news stories, such as the appointment of a new principal or the creation of a new curriculum. Panel programs may need student or educator participation, especially when they focus on children and youth. Occasionally, there are opportunities for public service announcements on special programs or community bulletin board shows.

Some stations have opportunities for guest editorial comments inserted in their newscasts. School personnel or community supporters should take this opportunity to deal with important or controversial issues.

Other concerns about relationships with television stations include getting from the station tapes of programs that would feature the school or its students. Another is providing volunteers or space for television station activities at the school site.

Finally, if people from the school are going to be involved on television, tape and critique presentations before the actual television appearance to prepare people to look good and behave naturally. The key to a successful television appearance is to be able to look in the camera and talk as though one is talking to one other person. A mistake many people make when they go on the electronic media is to act like some radio disc jockeys, yelling at all those people out there "in radio land" instead of relating one to one, to each individual viewer or listener.

Cable Television

Unlike broadcast television, cable television presents many great opportunities for the schools. More than two-thirds of the nation's homes have cable. As a result of their licensing agreements, virtually all cable operators have both public and educational access channels available for use by the schools. Cable channels also have available, at no cost, production facilities and training for people to do public or educational access programming on the station.

The staff and administration of the school can use cable television in many ways. The superintendent, principal, or headmaster can have a regular program discussing educational issues or presenting activities that are going on in the school. Board meetings can be broadcast on cable. Some public school districts have successfully used this technique, including the opportunity for call-in at public participation time during the board meetings.

Interview shows are relatively easy to produce. Dealing with subjects or personalities of interest to the public can be done well by school systems in a relatively efficient manner. Schools may want to sponsor call-in shows on identified hot education topics to help get ideas from the community and to assess the nature and intensity of community feelings.

School systems that have had difficulty getting the public to read the school's annual report have started either supplementing or replacing the print report with a video report. This video report can be broadcast on cable television repeatedly and then made available for presentation to other groups in the community.

Another use of cable television is the bulletin board, which can be used to display anything from the hot lunch menu to a list of student activities to telephone numbers of key people in the school system.

Student use of cable is limited only by the imagination of the students, subject to the general control of the school system to see that things are done in good taste. Students can produce programs in classes or as extracurricular activities. Student activities and game contests can be broadcast on cable's access channels to make those activities available to people who otherwise could not see them.

One cable issue that should also be addressed is the concern that cable has so little market penetration in terms of actual viewership. Most households with television sets in the United States now have cable, so it is accessible. How, then, does one get people to watch public access or educational access channels? The school must do a good job of publicizing what will be aired and of having regular program times so that an audience can grow over a period of time.

For example, it would be naive to assume a large audience for the school's annual report if it is simply put on cable without any advance promotion. The annual report is an example of something that can be publicized well in advance, with its broadcast schedule listed in newspapers and newsletters, in materials taken home by students, and on the cable television channel's schedule itself. It can be made even more available by encouraging people to make copies of the videotape from the cable broadcast.

Schools can use the public access channels for exchange programs with other communities, thus getting more material on local channels. Problem curriculum areas can be dealt with by putting special help programs on the local cable channel, such as a program for parents that gives them suggestions on how to help their child develop mathematics skills. In communities with many non–English-speaking parents, programs broadcast to parents in their native language can help them understand the school program and how they might work with their children on schoolwork.

Radio

Local radio presents many opportunities for school systems. In large metropolitan areas with many stations, because of market segmentation there is usually at least one station that would have some interest in school activities. In smaller communities that have one or two radio stations of their own, it is very easy for schools to get information on the radio.

Owners of small radio stations (and newspapers) often see themselves primarily as businesspeople who just happen to be in the media business. They usually need outside help in gathering news. Some small station newscasts are referred to as "rip-and-read," meaning that they literally rip articles out of newspapers and read them on the air for news. In these small operations, schools frequently can get their materials on the air merely by submitting information to the station.

Opportunities in radio include public service programs that usually run at times when not many people are listening (e.g., early Sunday morning). However, local stations will broadcast school news stories, cover sports events, and run public service announcements about upcoming activities.

The surest way to get a program on the radio is to have the program sponsored. Usually, the station has staff to get sponsors. If the station cannot find a sponsor for the school programming, the school might be able to identify and recruit a sponsor. Sometimes the radio stations themselves will even sponsor school programs.

Radio has interview shows, call-in shows, and occasionally opportunities for editorial comments. One way that many radio stations help schools is by announcing school closings or emergencies. These announcements are important things for a radio station because they ensure a listenership, at least at certain times.

It is important to remember that material presented on radio should be written in conversational language. Some of the best-written material sounds awkward on radio because it is not written to be read aloud in a casual, conversational way. When appearing on the radio, as on television, talk naturally as though interacting with one person. Stay away from jargon and aim the programming appropriately at the station's market. For example, if the station serves just one geographic area of a large school district, presentation should be of interest to the people in that area. It is important to know whether a station deals with a specific audience (e.g., youth, a particular ethnic or language group) or features specific programming (e.g., rock music, all talk).

Keep radio material brief and focused. An example is to produce something related to local history, such as the "history minute" type of programming that could be of interest to the radio station and a good project for students in the school.

To be effective in radio, there should be multiple voices, not just one individual droning on at length. The voices should be distinguishable from one another and should be pleasant. If materials are going to be recorded, use quality recorders and rooms that are appropriate so that there is no extraneous background noise. Music can be used very effectively in introducing or concluding or as background on radio.

Newspapers

There are many different ways to get material into newspapers. The first thing that has to be considered is the type of newspaper. Is it a daily newspaper that reaches a much larger area than is served by the school, is it a small weekly paper for a particular small town or neighborhood, or is it a paper geared to a specific ethnic or racial population?

Once one knows the circulation and audience of the paper and how it relates to the area served by the school district, then an effective approach can be determined.

Eight Ways to Get into the Newspapers **1. *News stories.*** Straight news stories written about activities at the school or people connected with the school are clearly one of the best ways to get into the newspapers. News stories submitted to a small local paper are very likely to get published since these papers typically depend on outside people to present them with much of their materials. News stories submitted to large daily papers are likely to either be reworked completely by the staff or not run at all, as the papers have professional pride in developing their own news stories.

One should not be discouraged if all stories submitted are not run. Politicians say that if you submit enough articles, something may get run. That is the basis on which they operate, and it may be a reasonable for a school, too.

2. Feature stories. As opposed to straight news stories (e.g., how many kids started school this year or the percentage of those who passed the statewide tests), features deal with something unique and interesting that would not be considered so-called hard news. Examples are the student doing an unusual project for a class, a teacher who had an interesting summer vacation activity, or remembrances of an old part of the building that is being torn down. Features are limited only by the creativity of the people who write them, and they can present the soft or warm side of your institution.

3. Columns. Weekly newspapers or newspapers serving special populations, neighborhoods, or small towns frequently allow someone from the school to run a column in the paper on a regular basis. Some examples are a principal writing a column about the major activities as the school year progresses, a fine arts teacher reviewing plays and movies, an agriculture teacher writing tips on gardening, and a counselor writing a column on getting prepared for employment or higher education. Whatever the subject, if someone connected to the school is writing the column, it can help build the image of the school in the community.

4. Student papers. If the school can't afford to publish its own student newspaper, some small town or neighborhood papers will periodically allow one or more of its pages to be set aside as the local student paper.

5. Editorials. In many smaller papers, the editors do not have the time or the inclination to write editorials of their own, but they may take sample editorials that are sent to them by newspaper publishers' associations or by interest groups. The school could be one of these interest groups sending sample editorials to the paper.

One example is an editorial suggesting the importance of parents working with students on homework and developing positive attitudes toward school. Others could deal with the importance of passing a referendum to support a new school building, a raise in the spending limits for the school district, or the importance of establishing a school–police liaison officer program.

6. Op-ed pieces. For large-circulation papers or for local paper editorials, there is the opportunity for the so-called op-ed piece. This allows an outsider to submit a signed editorial that would be presented not in the newspaper's normal editorial spot but somewhere else on the editorial page or the page opposite.

7. *Letters to the editor.* Another way in which the schools can get opinion material into the newspaper is through letters to the editor. It may be important for the school leader, a teacher, a school booster, or a group of students to write letters to the editor to clear up misconceptions or to let people know about interesting or unusual activities going on at the school. Letters to the editor should not be underestimated. They are usually one of the most highly read areas of a newspaper. Any credible letter to the editor must be signed, and the author must be identifiable in case the editor needs to verify the authenticity or check the facts of the letter.

8. *Advertising.* If all else fails, one way to get a message in the paper is to use paid advertising. School expenditures for advertising may be illegal in some areas and could be attacked as an inappropriate use of public funds in other places, but advisory committees, parents groups, booster clubs, and others might be willing to run ads if there is no other way to convey important school information through the news media.

SUGGESTED ACTIVITIES

1. Identify members of the school community who have skills to help with the public relations program: the ability to write good news and feature stories or to speak well on radio and television.
2. Develop a plan to get information about any outstanding or unusual activities by students or staff of the school.
3. Identify all the local news media and make preliminary contacts with each one before there is a need to meet with them.
4. As part of a crisis management plan, lay out the priorities and responsibilities for dealing with the public.
5. Conduct periodic surveys and/or focus groups to determine the public awareness of the school's programs and the accuracy of the information the public is receiving.
6. Build internal communications systems so that all employees and students have prompt and accurate information about school activities and issues.
7. Identify times and places in the community where the public can come to communicate directly with school officials.
8. Develop a list of all community organizations that have regular meetings with programs or speakers. Make available to those organizations a list of students and staff who could speak or perform for the organizations.

9. Offer to write a column for the local or neighborhood newspaper.
10. Develop a school program for local radio or cable television.

REFERENCE

American Association of School Administrators. (1950). *Public Relations for America's Schools*. Washington, D.C.: American Association of School Administrators.

RESOURCES

National Cable Television Association, 1724 Massachusetts Avenue NW, Washington, D.C. 20036. Telephone: 202-775-3669. Web: <http://www.ncta.com>.
National School Public Relations Association, 15948 Deerwood Road, Rockville, Maryland 20855. Telephone: 301-519-0496. Web: <http://www.nspra.org>.
Public Relations Society of America, 33 Irving Place, New York, New York 10003-2376. Telephone: 212-995-2230. Web: <http://www.prsa.org>.

9

CREATING EDUCATIONAL OPPORTUNITIES THROUGH PARTNERSHIPS

Partnerships with external entities provide opportunities to get resources, expand curricula, and excite students far beyond the ability of the school by itself. A *partnership* is a relationship in which each party provides something and each gains something. School partnerships probably have existed from the time the first school was created, but only recently have there been concerted efforts to create and utilize partnerships to deliver the educational program.

SEVEN MYTHS ABOUT PARTNERSHIPS

Before discussing the issues related to building partnerships, it is necessary to debunk some of the myths relating to this topic. These myths hinder the ability to develop the breadth, depth, and duration of partnerships possible for schools.

1. *Only the schools benefit.* As the definition of *partnership* makes clear, a partnership exists only if each party benefits from the relationship. If a school creates what it calls partnerships without any idea of what the other parties have to gain, it will and should be a tough sell.

Part of the reason for this myth is some of the terminology used in working with partners. The classic example is "Adopt a School." In communities such as St. Louis or Dallas, this term has been used for years and has a meaning well known, understood, and respected. However, for other communities, "Adopt a

School" can have a very negative connotation. To the school personnel, it appears that they will be in a subservient relationship. To the external partner, it may seem that they will be expected to take care of the adoptee.

2. A partnership must be a one-to-one relationship. This may be the easiest type of partnership to establish (e.g., one school building with one business), but it certainly is not the only possibility. In the next section of this chapter, it will be seen that the kinds of potential players and their configuration in partnerships are virtually unlimited.

3. There is only one right process to use in creating partnerships. This myth has its roots in the fact that some educators are so focused on process that they forget the goal of the activity. When the U.S. Department of Education first established an office on partnerships, a steady stream of education consultants came in, each claiming to have a process that would lead to successful partnerships. All the processes and their associated costs were different, but all the consultants were certain that theirs was the only way.

A large problem in partnering with business is that educators tend to focus on process and businesspeople on outcomes (i.e., "the bottom line"). Solid partnerships are based on two or more groups getting together to deal with *a shared concern.* The focus must be on the objective first. Once there is agreement on that, then and only then should the process be determined.

4. All that schools want is money. Unfortunately, in many cases this is true, but this narrow attitude stands in the way of building successful relationships. For example, a business leader in California once explained to a federal official that the local schools had asked him to raise a substantial sum of money from the other businesses in the area for general support of the schools. The business leader was willing, but he said that his associates were then rebuffed in their request to look at the books of the affected schools!

Obviously, schools create partnerships to expand their resources for serving learners. Cash is only one of those resources. Others include equipment, supplies, and personnel. Some examples are a business that is not be able to contribute cash to the school and so donates three-year-old computers, banks that give checkbooks and related materials to schools and assist the schools in teaching children how to use checking accounts, and a business that loans its strategic planning personnel to a school system to facilitate the school's own strategic plan.

5. Only big business can be partners. This myth is easy to explain. Bigger businesses have public relations staffs that do a good job of publicizing their community service efforts. Small businesses, such as the small-town Main Street merchant or the neighborhood shopkeeper in the city, do not have staff or publications to let the public know of all their activities. Small businesses are frequent partners with schools, but they rarely keep records of it. They just do "what comes naturally."

A secondary-school principal in a small town in Wisconsin was lamenting the lack of partnership opportunities because there was no big business in his community. With a little prodding, in less than one hour he managed to think of over seventy different ways that local businesses and organizations were involved with his school. While much of the involvement was small in scope, it still showed a willingness to support the schools. Providing convertibles for the homecoming parade, giving scrap lumber for use in shop classes, purchasing advertising in the yearbook (how many sales result from looking at a yearbook twenty years later?), speaking at career days, and periodically providing a page in the local newspaper for student news are examples of things commonly done.

6. *Only big school systems with special staff can create partnerships.* This myth exists for the same reason as the previous one: Large school systems have staff and publications to tell their story. Creating partnerships usually is easier for smaller schools because there is less bureaucracy. Several levels of approval may be required before entering into a relationship in a large system, while one quick call is often all that is necessary in the small school.

7. *Schools will lose control if they form community partnerships.* Traditional administrators are afraid that they will give up some of their power if partners become involved with the schools. It should be pointed out the schools already have two partners who dramatically curtail the authority of the local school leader: the federal and the state government.

Unlike the relationship between the federal and state governments, community partnerships are entirely voluntary. No school is forced to enter into any arrangement not of its liking. If a proposed partnership is not 100 percent satisfactory to the school, either it can be reworked to make it agreeable or the school can reject it. The school holds all the aces.

However, school leaders who are philosophically opposed to shared decision making may not want to enter into partnerships. Successful partnerships are based on mutual respect and trust, not on control.

WHO CAN BE PARTNERS?

Making an exhaustive list of potential partners is virtually impossible. One needs to create categories and then list local entities for each list. The following sections discuss some typical categories.

Business

This includes major employers, local franchises, local small business, and cottage industries. The chamber of commerce or commercial club should be able to provide the basic list. Check the business pages of the telephone directory for additional ideas.

Do not overlook any business. Sometimes partnerships come from the least expected places. For example, a major business partner with the public school located in the Mall of America is Browning-Ferris Industries (BFI). BFI, which provides the waste disposal for the mall, developed an environmental education program for the school, provides employment for students in a mall store, and made a ten-year commitment of $100,000 per year for support for the school.

Postsecondary Institutions

Research universities, liberal arts colleges, and teacher training institutions all are possible partners. Because of their local ties and entrepreneurial spirit, community colleges and technical colleges are usually agreeable to joint activities.

Both public and private institutions should be considered. One often-overlooked category is the for-profit or proprietary trade school. Whatever school is considered, be sure to see that it is accredited by the appropriate accrediting agency.

Some school–college partnerships are obvious. For example, a research university that does a study in a school enables the school to get needed information and the university students to get needed research experience.

Another example is the placement of teacher education students in observation, student teaching, and internship situations. Again, the college students get needed experience while the school gets an infusing of staff assistance and possibly new ideas or approaches.

Because of their clientele and local focus, the community and technical colleges and private trade schools may provide special opportunities for the schools to build partnerships dealing with at-risk students. Creating opportunities for students who have not succeeded in secondary schools is often part of the mission of these "open enrollment" institutions.

Other Schools

Partnerships between public schools in one district can lead to expanded curricular offering or the sharing of staff expertise. The same would apply to partnerships with other public school systems.

While not as common, public–private school partnerships have been beneficial to both. Prior to the recent emphasis on service learning in the public schools, there were numerous instances of Catholic high schools providing volunteers in public schools. These students were fulfilling the service requirements of their religion classes.

Day care and early childhood programs are not always seen as schools, but they almost always have some educational dimension. The types of relationships can be as diverse as providing realistic experiences for students in family life classes to giving elementary students esteem-building opportunities by reading to younger children.

Public and Nonprofit Human Service Agencies

Policy makers and pundits are demanding better integration of human services, including education. Budgets, administrative structures, union contract, and tradition are typical barriers to that integration. The schools can show good-faith attempts at integration by building partnerships with others. Agencies concerned with health, welfare, recreation, youth, alcohol/drug rehabilitation, law enforcement, and court services may be included on a list of potential partners.

Partnerships are very common with some of these groups. For example, recreational organizations often are feeder systems for varsity athletic programs, police cooperate with schools on the D.A.R.E. program, and public health nurses serve schools that do not have adequate health services of their own.

Less obvious partnerships can be developed. For example, school systems and the judge of the local juvenile court cooperated to attack teenage smoking. The problem was that only the schools attempted to enforce the law against underage smoking. By working with the judge, an agreement was reached to establish a ticket system. Every time a student was caught smoking, a ticket was issued with an appropriate penalty for each offense. Only after a specified number of offenses were dealt with by the school was there a petition to the juvenile court. Then the judge, who knew exactly what had led up to that point, would apply a judicial penalty. The schools got support they never had before, and the judge no longer had to be concerned with inconsistent behaviors on the part of school officials.

Community Groups

Americans are active joiners. Each community has its own diverse groups who have organizations for every interest and needs. Because of the unique nature of some groups, there usually is not one list that covers all types: civic, service, fraternal, religious, youth, and senior citizens, and so forth. School leaders should try to determine the number and nature of local organizations by using local directories and having brainstorming sessions with faculty and staff to ascertain their memberships and affiliations.

Partnerships can be made easily with organizations such as the Jaycees, Lions Club, Rotary, Kiwanis, and others whose goal is to provide community service. It takes more thought to develop mutually beneficial relationships with senior citizen groups.

Churches are an interesting challenge and a great opportunity in community partnerships. Concern about church–state issues in the curriculum has led some public schools to treat churches as though they do not exist. However, this need not be the case, as is shown by the very successful "Children First" initiative in St. Louis Park, Minnesota, a partnership among schools, churches, business, health, and city government.

Government

This category overlaps somewhat with the others, particularly in the human service areas. However, there are other agencies of government at all levels that can partner with local schools, including federal, state, county, city, township, and special units of government.

In Washington, D.C., the federal government is *the* business in town. One elementary school that achieved the "Blue Ribbon" award from the U.S. Department of Education was cited for the effective way in which federal employees worked with young children. Scientists and researchers from various agencies gave demonstrations and developed projects with the students.

Another kind of partnership is one in which the schools cooperate with transportation authorities to save education expenses and to increase ridership in public transportation.

Several state legislatures cooperate with the schools by providing educational and work experiences at the state capitol. This gives the students a real-world knowledge of government while getting some work done for the legislature.

WHY EVERYONE WINS WITH SCHOOL–BUSINESS PARTNERSHIPS

Most discussions of school partnerships focus on the relationship with business. Before attempting to establish a partnership with business, it would be good to review the reasons why it is mutually beneficial. Brown and Scherer (1984) identified twelve reasons why businesses want school partners and twelve reasons why schools should want business partners. Those reasons are summarized in table 9.1.

As educational and business leaders sit down together, they can review these reasons and see which might best characterize their situation. In most cases, the schools are looking for resources (money, equipment, supplies, personnel), but sometimes the most important outcome of the relationship would be to build community support for future referenda.

Each of the reasons listed in the table has been applied many times in successful partnerships. For example, a partnership with a "school to work" emphasis would help business get better entry-level employees and influence career choice while the school would be getting contacts for career programs and job placements.

With the advent of the accountability movement and changes in delivery systems and organizational structure, schools with limited staff development budgets may have a need for management expertise and staff development assistance that could be provided by a partner who has gone through the same type of changes.

The public relations and tax benefits are obvious to most businesses. A school looking for partners can identify businesses who have a public relations need (e.g., a power plant that releases pollutants into the air or water) and use that as a basis for beginning conversations.

Technology companies developing software and hardware can do beta testing in a school. This could provide the school with equipment and curricular or administrative software.

One of the surest ways to build a partnership is to focus on economic education, the only reason that appears on both lists in the table. Many schools know that they need help in teaching both micro- and macroeconomics, and many businesses are frustrated with the lack of knowledge of our economic system, a clear case of a common concern.

Some businesses would just like to be good citizens. This reason is not obvious to the educators, but, just like individuals, not all businesses are alike. The

Table 9.1   Reasons for School–Business Partnerships

Business Reasons	School Reasons
public relations	money
tax benefit	obtain equipment
better entry-level employees	obtain supplies
develop markets	additional personnel
develop products	staff development
influence career choice	management expertise
recruit employees	add variety; enrich program
economic education	economic education
develop better citizens	contacts for jobs and programs
make a profit	show good faith and openness
improve employee morale	provide additional role models
be a good citizen	build community support

alert educator who identifies businesses that have a strong sense of community service has great partnership possibilities.

VOLUNTEERS: THE IDEAL PARTNERS

Virtually everyone agrees that parents and schools must be partners if students are to get the maximum benefit from their educational opportunities. While parents are most important, each individual who volunteers to work with the school is a partner in the educational enterprise. These personal partnerships not only help the students but also develop a sense of loyalty and support for the school system. A successful volunteer program depends on an understanding of the program's elements and who can be school volunteers.

Volunteer Program Elements

All successful volunteer programs have seven common elements. In informal settings, the elements may not be spelled out, but they are there. When starting a volunteer program, list the following elements and determine who is responsible for each, how it will be carried out, and the timetable for conducting the activities:

1. *Recruitment.*   In starting a new program, consider recruiting in the spring for the following school year. This will yield a cadre of key volunteers to help establish and maintain the program. While the big push is for the opening of school, recruiting should be an ongoing activity. Assume that everyone is a potential volunteer. Use your marketing and public relations skills and sources mentioned in chapters 7 and 8 to help you develop a comprehensive recruitment program. Once you have identified potential talent pools, the simplest and most effective way to get volunteers is to *ask* them. Polls consistently show that the number-one reason people volunteer is that someone asked them. For example, in a 1999 survey by Independent Sector (2000), almost 90 percent of the respondents said that they would volunteer if asked.

2. *Orientation.*   Before volunteers begin, they need some basic orientation to the facilities, the program, the personnel, and the rules of your school. Of utmost importance is an explanation of data privacy laws and procedures to be followed in case of emergencies. The roles and limits of the volunteers should be made clear. Each volunteer should know whom to contact if the supervisor is not available.

3. *Placement.*   This is most crucial to the success of a program. Placing volunteers in situations in which they are fearful, have no interest in the ac-

tivity, or have personality conflicts will drive them away and jeopardize the entire program.

Effective placement involves identifying the needs of the program, asking the potential supervisors and volunteers to identify their interests, and matching people and program on the basis of needs and interests. On rare occasions, a placement does not work out. In that case, a change in placement needs to be made as soon as possible to avoid negative feelings by the parties and serious harm to the program.

4. Training. If you do not have time to train everyone involved, train the supervisors first, then the volunteers. Well-trained supervisors can and will train the volunteers. If the volunteer is doing simple tasks, such as stapling or collating papers, the training can be accomplished with a few comments. More complex tasks may require ongoing training. Effective training is a sound investment of time that will yield work dividends beyond your greatest expectations. Whenever possible, put the training in writing.

5. Supervision. To benefit the volunteers and to accomplish the goals of the program, volunteers must be supervised. Supervisors who are committed will lead to a successful program, so use only willing supervisors. Working with volunteers will initially increase the workload of the supervisor, but in a short time the volunteers will be assuming much of the load previously done by the professional. Depending on the nature of the activity, supervisors need not always be present when volunteers are carrying out their duties.

6. Evaluation. All facets of the program should be evaluated. Volunteers should be evaluated by supervisors and supervisors evaluated by volunteers. The entire program should be evaluated by participants and beneficiaries (usually teachers, students, and parents). Simple one-page evaluation checklists are available, such as those developed by Suzanne Taranto (1983), the former director of the School Volunteer Office for the Florida, in her book *Coordinating Your School Volunteer Program.*

7. Recognition. One of the great joys of using school volunteers is the recognition program. This can be anything from a simple thank-you and a certificate to an elaborate reception or dinner with levels of recognition based on amount, type, and length of volunteer service. An effective recognition program might include immediate responses to the volunteer activity; ongoing recognition through newsletters, posters, and so forth; and an annual recognition event. Developing and operating recognition programs can be a wonderful opportunity for staff and volunteers to exercise their creativity.

An example of a recognition program with great impact on the volunteers and the public was the statewide program in Florida that brought outstanding volunteers to a special day at Disney World.

Who Are Volunteers?

When T. H. Bell was the U.S. secretary of education, he sent a letter to all the nation's school superintendents suggesting that they start school volunteer programs if they did not already have them. A reply from the superintendent of a sizable, affluent suburban district said, "You don't know what you are talking about, 'those women' have all gone to work."

That superintendent was caught up in the myth that only upper-income full-time homemakers are volunteers. In fact, volunteers come from all segments of our society—male and female, young and old, affluent and poor, employed outside the home and not employed—and from all racial and ethnic groups. Two of the best sources of volunteers for a school are senior citizens and the students in the school system.

Polls done for Independent Sector consistently show that over half the people in the United States do some volunteering each year. The most recent poll indicated that 56 percent of adults over eighteen years of age volunteered in 1999.

Who Benefits from Volunteering?

While religion is the number-one beneficiary of American voluntarism, education is usually second, followed closely by the health field. In 1995, for example, 25 percent of all volunteers did church work, and about 18 percent volunteered in schools, according to the U.S. Census Bureau (1999) in the *Statistical Abstract of the United States*. Also of importance to educators is that another 15 percent of the population volunteered in the field of youth development.

The Psychology of a Successful Volunteer Program

The mechanics of operating a program are important, but it is even more important to remember that the participants are human beings and should be treated as such.

When people initially participate, they often are hesitant or tentative. Make them feel comfortable. Remember that many people have misconceptions about today's schools that are based on rumors or media reports of incidents that may have occurred anywhere in the country. Provide a friendly environment with name tags, refreshments, and available resource people to answer questions.

Tom Kelly, manager of the Minnesota Twins, has won two world championships with teams that had few superstars. Kelly won by using all his players and placing each one of them in situations where he was most likely to succeed. This philosophy can be applied to volunteer programs as well. To maximize potential success, let people choose their own activities from the list you have. Once they are involved with the program, it is possible and likely that you can get them to do other or additional activities. This is because the person gains confidence and also develops a commitment to the school—it becomes "our school" to the volunteers.

A sense of belonging is crucial to the success of the program. It is even more important to the individual, as the volunteer activity fulfills that basic psychological need to be needed.

In one situation, a group of senior citizens in a nursing home were recruited to do some simple envelope stuffing. Even though they would be in an elementary school, they were fearful because of what they believed was the unruly nature of kids in modern schools. Finally, several people did agree to volunteer since they would be in a group and would be working in a room by themselves. In a short time, they began to enjoy themselves, and others joined them.

One day a teacher stopped in the workroom and explained that she had a student who had missed several days of school and needed someone to read to him. One volunteer finally agreed to venture into the classroom to help the student. The volunteer got so enthused about the experience that soon several others were in classrooms working on reading with other students. By the end of the year, almost the entire group of seniors who had started in the workroom were out in classrooms helping teachers, and an entire new group of their colleagues had come from the nursing home to do the tasks in the workroom.

Independent Sector surveys indicate that 43 percent of seniors age 75 and older have participated in volunteering. This indicates that the pool of potential volunteers is large and growing in an aging population. It also shows the importance to many people of being active and contributing to society.

In many instances, the primary beneficiary of volunteering is the volunteer himself. The opportunity to feel good about oneself by doing for others cannot be overstated. For example, during the 1980s, VOLUNTEER, a national organization dedicated to promoting voluntarism, conducted a program in which physically handicapped individuals carried out volunteer projects. For many of the participants, it was the first time they had the opportunity to do something for others rather than having others do something for them.

Building self-esteem is greatly emphasized in the American educational system, but not until the relatively recent emphasis on service learning has voluntarism been seen as part of that effort. Also, too often the students most in need of a boost in a feeling of self-worth are treated only as victims and not as ones who can contribute through their own voluntary efforts.

TRENDS IN EDUCATION PARTNERSHIPS

With an increased emphasis on education partnerships in the 1990s, several trends have emerged that are reshaping attitudes about the types, usefulness, and value of these relationships:

1. *There is less panic by educators.* In the past, the suggestion that "outsiders" would be in the schools or helping give direction to the school or some of its programs often was met with educator anxiety or hostility.
2. *More school systems are initiating partnerships.* Through the creation of school foundations and partnership programs and by establishing positions of partnership coordinators, schools are reaping the benefits of community partnerships. Even when the system has no formal partnership program, individual administrators and teachers are being encouraged to use their own initiative in establishing partnerships.
3. *Recognition programs are growing in number and visibility.* Government, business, education, and the news media all are players in recognizing outstanding programs. From national programs, such as the Points of Light Foundation, to individual principal's awards, recognition is being given to those who contribute to schools through partnerships and voluntarism.
4. *Expectations are becoming more realistic.* Partnership and volunteer programs are no longer being seen as panaceas. Both schools and the community have come to realize that partnerships may supplement and enhance the educational program, but they do not provide a comprehensive program themselves.
5. *There is a more substantial and essential involvement of the nonschool partners.* Their role is seen as an integral part of a comprehensive community school offering. Less emphasis is on band-aids and more emphasis is on activities such as strategic planning and total quality management (TQM).
6. *Partnerships are becoming more complex.* An increasing number of partners, a greater variety of partners, and multidistrict partnerships are all indications of this trend.
7. *Business is getting involved with the schools at all levels: national, state and local.* At the local level, business is working with school districts, buildings, and individual classes. The Business Roundtable (BRT), the U.S. Chamber of Commerce, the National Federation of Independent Business (NFIB), and the National Alliance of Business (NAB) are all national business organizations working with education.

8. *Business is getting more involved in educational policy.* The BRT is composed of the chief executive officers of many of the biggest corporations in the country. It made a ten-year commitment to influence educational policy in the United States and has since extended that commitment. Comparable state-level organizations are using high-level partnerships in working on educational policy. For example, in Iowa the business leadership worked with labor, agriculture, and educational leaders to develop common educational goals and programs.

9. *More educational partnerships are operating outside the traditional school settings.* Charter schools, alternative learning centers, and storefront public schools are examples of this trend.

10. *The emphasis is now on systemic change.* The creation of the New American Schools Development Corporation, the emphasis on co-location and integration of services, and the partnerships involving higher education and professional organizations are all part of this trend.

TIPS ON BUILDING PARTNERSHIPS AND PROGRAMS

1. *Assess where the school is and start there.* The number and range of activities developed by individual administrators, teachers, coaches, and others often surprise educational leaders who have no formal programs.

2. *Build on common needs.* Ask what are the community needs, determine the role the school could play in meeting some of those needs, and decide what kind of activity would make everyone a winner. For example, a partnership to reduce shoplifting saves money for merchants, helps the schools with civic education, and may keep some young people from having a criminal record.

3. *Do not get hung up on differences.* There may be a tendency to dismiss as possible partners businesses or individuals with whom the school or its staff have had differences, for example, the newspaper that opposed a referendum, an oil refinery that is seen as a source of pollution, or the private school that competes for students. By focusing on common needs instead of differences, the school will build partnerships and model positive conflict resolution behaviors.

4. *Distinguish between short-term and long-term needs.* Dealing with an ad hoc or short-term problem can provide a trial run for new partnerships. If it proves successful, then a long-term relationship might be created. An example is a school ecology class working with community organizations on a cleanup project that then can lead to a full-scale recycling program.

5. *Start slowly, then build on successes.* Never force anyone to participate. Most adults have a reluctance to try new things. Work first with the most venturesome staff and community people. With a properly developed program, the overwhelming majority of the school employees and many other community folks will join in when they see success and possible personal benefits. Ignore the malcontents, and they will eventually isolate themselves.

6. *Check out the legal and insurance issues.* Many states have hold-harmless provisions and workers' compensation provisions to protect volunteers and partners in school. If not, see that insurance (provided by either the school or a partner) covers everyone involved in partnerships on or off the school site.

7. *Make sure that all the appropriate officials know of and, if necessary, approve all programs.* Nothing is more embarrassing and irritating to a business leader, school administrator, or other organizational leader than to have a program existing under them of which they are not aware.

SUGGESTED ACTIVITIES

1. Take an inventory of the partnership and volunteer activities now being conducted in the school.
2. Identify issues that concern the school, but are not exclusively school problems.
3. List existing community relationships.
4. List reasons why the school would benefit from community partnerships and reasons why businesses and organizations might want to be a partner with the school.
5. List organizations from which you could recruit volunteers.
6. Canvas the school for both administrative and classroom settings where volunteers or partner resources could contribute to the mission and program of the school.
7. Establish ties with postsecondary educational institutions (both academic and vocational) based on common needs and concerns.
8. Contact the state office of volunteer services and local volunteer centers to make use of their materials and programs.
9. Periodically check the Web sites of national resources listed at the end of this chapter.

REFERENCES

Brown, Robert J., and Scherer, Joseph J. (1984). Businesses and school: Reasons for a partnership. *Journal of Career Education* 10:197–203.

Independent Sector. (2000). *Giving and volunteering in the United States, 1999 Edition.* <http://www.independentsector.org>, April 21.

Taranto, Suzanne. (1983). *Coordinating your school volunteer program.* Palo Alto, Calif.: Vort Corporation.

U.S. Census Bureau. (1999). *Statistical Abstract of the United States.* 119th ed. Washington, D.C.: U.S. Government Printing Office.

RESOURCES

National Association of Partners in Education, 901 North Pitt Street, Alexandria, Virginia 22314. Telephone: 703-836-4880. Web: <http://www.partnersineducation.org>.

Points of Light Foundation, 1400 I Street, Washington, D.C. 20005. Telephone: 202-729-8000. Web: <http://www.pointsoflight.org>.

10

SEEKING AND SECURING GRANTS

Americans are very generous people. According to the AAFRC Trust for Philanthropy, charitable giving in the United States was over $190 billion in 1999. Of that money, almost 80 percent was given by individuals. The rest was given by corporations, foundations, and bequests.

Competition for these discretionary dollars can be fierce, but opportunities do exist for individuals and schools that have a sense of mission and the understanding of the techniques of successful fund-raising.

This discussion of securing major grants is divided into three parts: proposal writing, foundations, and government sources. Chapter 11 presents a variety of techniques for raising money from local sources.

PROPOSAL WRITING

To secure money from both government sources and foundations, it is necessary to understand some of the basic principles of proposal writing.

Some common pitfalls that need to be avoided are considering only one funder, writing by committee, and writing for the wrong reasons. The best way to avoid these pitfalls is to begin by writing a concept proposal.

What is to be accomplished? Who is going to do it? How is it to be done? The answers to these questions will yield a concept proposal. This proposal should demonstrate the passion of the authors in solving a problem or accomplishing a goal. Once a draft is completed, the proposal should be circulated among others not involved with the project to see whether it can be understood by independent readers.

There are seven basic elements that should be included in any grant proposal:

1. *Need statement.* The need should relate to the purpose of the school, it should be reasonable in scope, and it should be supported by evidence or statements from recognized authorities on the subject. It is helpful if the need statement is developed with input from those who might benefit from the proposed program. The need statement should be brief, interesting, and not contain any jargon. A well-written need statement should make a strong case for the proposed project and for the authors as the best persons to carry it out.

2. *Objectives.* The objectives should delineate clearly the outcomes expected from the proposal, who would benefit from the project, and the time line for implementation. It is important to have at least one objective for each need stated. The objectives should be measurable, and it is important to remember that such objectives are not methods but, rather, goals to be accomplished.

3. *Methods.* The methods should flow from the objectives of the program. The best methods should describe in detail the program and the reasons for the specific activities selected. The method section of the proposal should make clear who is being served, who is on the staff delivering the program, and the sequence of activities to accomplish the objectives.

4. *Personnel.* Selecting the right personnel is crucial to winning a grant. It must be made clear that the people offering the program have the background and competence to make it work. The most important person to the success of the proposal will be the project director. If this is not a credible individual, there is very little likelihood of receiving a grant. It is also important to provide the qualifications and job descriptions of other personnel who will have significant roles in the project.

In addition to the project personnel, there are several other related personnel issues that may be addressed in the proposal. For example, will any consultants be used? If so, why are they needed, and how will they be selected? Will there be an advisory committee or committees for the project? What is the need for these committees, and how are they selected? Advisory committees can be handy tools to build credibility for the project if potential funders do not know the applicants. An advisory committee can provide some "borrowed" credibility.

Compensation is another personnel issue. Should those working in the project be granted released time from their regular duties, should they be compensated on an overload basis, and how should the compensation relate to the normal pay? Most funders will not pay a salary greater than the individual would normally be earning, but they will pay for released time or overload work.

5. Budget.   The first issue with respect to budget is who the fiscal agent for the project will be. That is, who will be held accountable for financial management? This is a simple issue if the request is from one school, but it is much more complicated and needs to be clarified if there are other schools or partners involved.

It is important that the budget reflect the proposal as stated in the sections on need, objectives, methods, and evaluation. The budget should be stated with enough detail to be clearly understood. Is should include fringe benefits for employees and the costs of any consultants. In developing the budget, it is necessary to determine the policy of the funders concerning indirect costs or overhead. Some funders will allow no indirect costs. With others, it may be possible to get anywhere from 8 to 20 percent of the budget for overhead.

Another issue relates to cash and in-kind contributions. The budget should reflect all resources committed to the project not only from the external funder but also from the partners in the project. For example, will the budget include space, equipment, supplies, telephones, and other things provided by the school at no direct cost to the project? Will there be work done by volunteers to reduce the direct costs of the project? It is important to analyze all facets of the project and put a dollar value on every possible contribution. In this way, the funding agency will see that it is not the sole contributor to the budget.

6. Finance plan.   As was implied in the discussion on budget, the total real cost of the project is likely to be substantially more than the amount contributed by the grant. The finance plan should describe the other sources of funds, the amounts and kinds of soft-money matching, and the annual plans for financing the project until it is completed. The finance plan and the budget should be detailed year by year for the duration of the project.

Most agencies that give grants would like to see plans for the continued funding of the project after the grant money has been spent. Both government agencies and private foundations have limited resources for discretionary grants, so they are inclined to give their money for innovative projects. Then, if a new concept works, the grant-receiving institution is expected to continue with its own or other funds. For this reason, it is helpful to include a multiyear budget and finance plan that will show the eventual replacement of most or all of the grant money with funds from other sources if the program is to be ongoing. Typically, this plan should project costs and income for three years even though the proposal is for a one-year grant.

It is important to get letters of commitment from any individuals or entities that would be considered a source of funds or soft-money matching for the grant. It is also helpful to the proposal if some reference can be made to the track record of the school and project partners with previous grants.

7. Evaluation.   The lack of a clear and well-defined evaluation plan is one of the most common reasons that grant proposals fail. In developing the evaluation plan, it is important to go back over the need, objectives, and methods to see that there is internal consistency.

The evaluation plan should state what the criteria are for the success of the program, how the data will be gathered to determine success, and how the analysis of the data is to be done. If standardized tests or survey instruments are used, there should be some reference to their reliability and validity. If the evaluation instruments are developed for the specific project, there should be an explanation as to the appropriateness of the instruments and how they were developed.

Who is doing the evaluating is of great importance if the evaluation is subjective or qualitative. In this case, it should be explained how the evaluators were selected, what their qualifications are, and whether they are independent of the control of the school.

The proposal should include a plan for the development and dissemination of evaluation reports. Make clear how frequently and in what manner reports will be given to the funding agency. Determine who else should be given reports and the nature of those additional reports. After all the elements have been spelled out, it is then possible to write a *summary,* or *abstract,* to be used for discussion purposes. This also can be submitted with the final proposal if requested by the funder. In submitting a proposal, there should be a cover letter followed by the summary (which should be as hard hitting and direct as possible) followed by the seven proposal elements in order (unless the funder requests a different format).

FOUNDATIONS

The first inclination in dealing with foundations is to write a proposal and submit it to whatever foundation someone might be familiar with. This is almost certainly a recipe for disaster. To be effective in getting support from foundations, an analysis must be done about the types of foundations, the types of grants they give, and which fields the foundations give to.

Types of Foundations

The foundations that most people are aware of are the large *general-purpose foundations* that have a broad charter and a professional staff. These foundations might be national or international, such as the Ford Foundation, the Pew Charitable Trust, or the Rockefeller Foundation. Because of their size and long-standing reputations, these foundations are the first ones that most people think about when seeking funds. However, they are not usually good sources of support for local schools because they tend to support projects of national significance and because the amounts of money requested by local schools are less than the amounts usually given by these foundations.

Regional, state, or local general-purpose foundations are much better prospects for funding local schools. In many cases, these foundations have a specific geographic focus. If they also focus on education as a field of giving, then they are good prospects for possible funding.

Special-purpose foundations are limited by their charters to specific fields of giving, such as health, education, the fine arts, or social service. While the logical place for a school to start looking would be the education foundations, it would be a mistake to dismiss immediately other types of foundations as prospects. For example, an arts foundation may be helpful in getting funding for the music or theater programs at the school, and a health-related foundation might have interest in the school wellness program.

Community foundations provide support for a variety of activities within a defined geographic area, usually a city (and its suburbs) or possibly a state. Community foundations receive gifts from a variety of sources and distribute funds on the basis of perceived community needs. One big advantage in going to a community foundation is that it is more inclined to give support for ongoing programs than most other types of foundations. Also, the competition is usually less intense for funds from community foundations than from a national or regional general-purpose or even special-purpose foundation.

Another type of foundation is the *corporate foundation*. In this case, the company transfers money to its charitable giving arm. Sometimes a foundation is established with a large amount of company stock. Other corporate foundations receive transfer payments from the company each year, depending on the financial health of the corporation. Funds from corporate foundations usually go to communities where the company has employees or plants or where it does a large percentage of its business. Many corporate foundations give a substantial portion of their foundation dollars in the community in which the corporate headquarters is located. Foundations of major retail chains may make some contributions in any community in which they have a store.

One other type of foundation that should be mentioned is the *family foundation* that is established by living persons. Members of the family usually control the funds. Since many small family foundations tend to function on an informal basis, it is important to get to know the members if an appeal is to be made to one of these organizations. Some family foundations have community foundations administer their funds, but the family members may still retain substantial control over the grant-giving activities.

Types of Foundation Grants

Another way to view foundations is by the types of grants they give. Listed here are some of the common types of grants as specified by various foundations:

1. *Research grants*. Provided to individuals, groups, or organizations for research projects
2. *Training grants*. Provided to public or nonprofit groups for starting or improving training programs
3. *Service grants*. Provided to assist the operation of activities or programs
4. *Construction grants*. Provided for new construction of remodeling old buildings, to bring them up to date, or to alter them for different uses
5. *Demonstration grants*. Provided to start pilot projects or programs

The type of grants liked most by recipients of foundation funds are *institutional grants*, which are unrestricted and allow the school to use the money as it sees fit.

Fields of Giving

Most foundations, even general-purpose foundations, emphasize specific fields of giving. Major categories are education, religion, health and welfare, science, arts, and humanities. Within these broad categories are many areas of specialization.

For example, some education foundations are interested only in higher education, others in K–12, and others in vocational education. Some prefer private education, while others will contribute only to public schools. Some contribute only for specific purposes, such as endowments, libraries, staff development, scholarships, interinstitutional cooperation, or specific curricular areas, such as science.

Having a good understanding of the type of foundation, its fields of giving, and the type of grants it gives can save time and needless expenditure of energy on the part of those seeking funds for educational projects or programs.

WHAT FOUNDATIONS LOOK FOR IN A PROPOSAL

The first thing the foundation would consider is the appropriateness of the proposal to the foundation's purpose and current goals. Considered next would be the feasibility and realism of the project. The importance of the project to the community or to the recipients, its timeliness, the potential impact, and the originality may all affect the funding decision. Historically, foundations are more willing than government to fund high-risk, creative proposals. Is the project a model that can be replicated, if successful? Because foundations have limited resources, replicability gives it "more bang for the buck."

Two elements that may be examined closely are the budget and the evaluation plans. Does the budget adequately explain the need for funding, the local matching funds or in-kind contributions, and the long-range finance plans? Are the costs reasonable in relations to the benefits that might be gained? Will the evaluation show measurable results?

The ability of the applicant to carry out the project would be evaluated. This would include an evaluation of the competence of the personnel. Sometimes a foundation may like a proposal but may question whether the applicant is the one best suited to complete it. In that case, the foundation may recommend that the applicant form a partnership with a more experienced organization or else establish an advisory group to help guide the project.

STEPS IN SEEKING A FOUNDATION GRANT

1. Write a concept proposal and circulate it to all interested parties for review and comment.
2. Once there is agreement on the concept, establish responsibilities for the detailed proposal: determine functions to be accomplished, assign staff to the functions, and develop a time line for each function.
3. Develop a list of all foundations that might consider the proposal. The Foundation Center, a national nonprofit clearinghouse on foundations, is an excellent resource. Its Internet site has a wealth of information, some free and some requiring a fee. For example, it is possible to subscribe for one month for a fee of less than $20 to Foundation Directory Online, which provides information on over 10,000 foundations. If the school is going to use this resource on a regular basis, it is cheaper to get an annual subscription.

Affiliated with the Foundation Center are Cooperating Collections, located in public libraries or colleges in every state. By checking the Foundation Center's Web site, it is possible to find the nearest center. The centers are free resources that contain publications of interest to grant seekers, and some of the centers have the latest IRS filings of the private foundations in the state.

4. Prioritize the foundations on the basis of their purpose, size of grants, and recent pattern of giving.

5. Try to determine whether anyone connected with the school has a relationship with staff or board members of any of the prospective grantors. This could modify the priority list.

6. Establish contact with the foundation staff and maintain a relationship throughout the application process. Assign this task to one person so that the foundation does not get confused or get mixed signals from the school.

7. Write the final proposal after input from all participants. Do not use jargon or try to be cute. Proofread carefully to eliminate spelling or grammatical errors and recheck all financial data. Be sure to include all elements requested by the funder. Include letters of support.

8. Submit the proposal.

9. Follow up to see that everything is received and in proper order.

10. Learn from experience. Always seek feedback. Foundations are under no obligation to say why they decided which projects to fund, but it never hurts to ask. Usually, a formal letter informing an applicant that it was not successful simply says that there were many more worthy proposals than the foundation could fund. Conversations with foundation staff at that point might help.

FEDERAL FUNDING ISSUES

Discretionary grant money is available from many federal agencies. It is naive to think that the U.S. Department of Education is the only possible federal source of funds for school grants. In fact, the Department of Education has far less discretionary grant money than many other federal agencies.

Good grant writers are limited only by their imaginations in determining how their needs fit the programs of various government departments. Even within the Department of Education, a person in K–12 education should not forget less obvious sources, such as the Fund for the Improvement of Postsecondary Education (FIPSE). Many FIPSE grants are available to partnerships between higher-education institutions and schools.

Listed here are some of federal departments and agencies that in the past have given grants to schools and school-age children:

Department of Health and Human Services. Money is available from the National Institutes of Health, the National Institute of Mental Health, the Center for Disease Control, and the community service offices. The health-related agencies have been involved with a variety of health education projects, and community service block grants have been used for such things as funding the National Youth Sports Program, which provides summer athletic and academic activities for low-income youth.

National Endowment for the Humanities (NEH) and *National Endowment for the Arts (NEA).* Both are small agencies that fund programs related to teacher training and development of curriculum materials for schools. For example, the NEH has supported teacher training dealing with the Bill of Rights and other programs related to history and humanities. The NEA develops materials that can assist schools, particularly those who have limited arts curricula.

National Science Foundation. This agency usually has far more money for grants than does the Department of Education. While most of its programs fund scientists, higher education, and other organizations, it has been involved in the development of science curricula and training science teachers.

Department of Labor. There was a time when the Department of Labor had more money for training than the entire elementary and secondary education budget of the U.S. Department of Education. While that is no longer true, the recent emphasis on school-to-work programs has made Department of Labor a major partner with education and potential source of some support.

Department of Justice. For several years, the Department of Justice has been involved in law-related education. Justices also work with the Department of Education in partnerships concerning juvenile delinquency and crime prevention.

Department of Energy. Because it is so heavily dependent on scientists for the promotion and control of energy use, the Department of Energy has been involved with programs to interest youth in science and to develop their abilities in that field.

Department of Housing and Urban Development. Since the task of this department is to build communities, potential partnerships among housing agencies, schools, and other agencies are possible ways to get additional resources for the schools.

This list of federal agencies and some of the things they have done or might be willing to do is neither comprehensive nor exhaustive. After determining the school or community need to be met, creativity can be used in deciding which federal agencies should have the opportunity to participate in the project.

FEDERAL FUNDING TIPS

1. *Understand the differences between grants and contracts.* Grants are almost always made on a competitive basis, but contracts may or may not be competitive.
2. *Consider submitting an unsolicited proposal.* When the government solicits a request for proposal (RFP), it is inviting competition for a grant or contract. What is not so well known is that some federal monies are awarded to authors of unsolicited proposals. Successful unsolicited proposals are rare and usually are submitted by major national organizations. Nevertheless, this option might be considered for someone having a truly unique work or a special new program.
3. *Know the deadlines for federal grant requests.* A proposal must be received by the exact time specified in the request for proposal, or it will not be considered. Always allow enough time for proposals to reach the appropriate office. Normally, the RFP will specify the date when the proposal is due, and only proposals that are postmarked at least one week before the due date are accepted. Authors of major proposals have been known to hand carry the proposals to the appropriate office in Washington to ensure that the deadlines are met.
4. *Get the RFP as a soon as possible.* The sooner one gets the RFP, the sooner one can start developing the response. Frequently, the agencies cannot release the RFP until late in the fiscal year (they must wait until Congress and the president have agreed on the budget), so the time lines can be very short. To do preliminary planning, review RFPs from previous years since agencies generally do not make significant changes in RFPs from one year to the next. Have someone monitor the *Federal Register* in order to get the official RFP as soon as it is released in case there are significant changes from the previous year.
5. *Whenever possible, visit the program offices of the federal agencies that are potential sources of funds.* Visiting with program staff face to face provides the opportunity to get more detailed knowledge of what they want in grant proposals. The personal visit makes it easier to carry on extended conversations by phone or by Internet later. Building a relationship with

program officers does not ensure funding, but it may mean that they will help point out flaws in the proposal that can be corrected before final submission. Make use of the technical assistance of program staff whenever possible.

6. *Attend all possible meetings that relate to the grant program.* Briefings, program hearings, and meetings of directors of existing projects can yield information to help develop a better proposal that will have a greater likelihood of success.

7. *Follow instructions exactly.* If the RFP requires proposals to be submitted triple spaced with one-inch margins, do that exactly. Some people have outsmarted themselves by trying to make their proposals stand out by using colored paper, odd-size sheets of paper, and so forth. All this does is ensure the disqualification of the proposal.

8. *Get a copy of reviewers' comments.* Whenever a proposal is submitted to a federal agency, the authors have a right to see the comments of the reviewers after the competition. What authors get (only if requested) is a copy of the actual score sheets used with the name of the reviewer blocked out. This will show the points given for each part of the proposal and any additional comments of the reviewer. This information can be very helpful in the future.

9. *Become a program reader.* Submit a resume to the program office. There is always a need for readers. With the appropriate background, it is possible to be selected as a reader. Being a reader provides a better understanding of the process and can yield many new ideas that can then be used to develop proposals for other government or private funders. Also, in those situations when readers are brought together in Washington or at another site, the contacts made while rating proposals will enable one to network with successful project directors and can lead to future partnerships.

10. *Ask your congressional and senatorial offices to help you to follow up.* Do not expect pressure from the members of Congress, but they can be helpful in keeping track of the process and in getting information that may be useful for current or future requests.

11. *Be aware of year-end funds.* In a typical year, not all the appropriated money is spent. As the end of the fiscal year approaches, funds may become available. At this point, program officers sometimes have the authority to distribute small amounts (by federal standards) in the form of sole source (noncompetitive) contracts or purchase orders. Those in regular contact with the program office are more likely to get some money this way in response to a brief proposal. Because of the amount

of money involved, these proposals need not be subject to the normal grant process.

12. *Do not go to the federal government for the small stuff.* With the exception of the previously mentioned year-end funds, it is usually not worth the effort to go to federal government for small grants. The amount of money that may be received should always be judged against the amount of time, effort, and resources devoted to the proposal process.

SUGGESTED ACTIVITIES

1. Survey staff, students, and community members for needs and wants. Create a wish list and then prioritize it.
2. Using the resources of the foundation center, identify ten foundations and collect annual reports and other information about them. Most foundations now have Web sites, so this is much easier to do now than it was in the past.
3. Designate an individual to monitor the *Federal Register* and the U.S. Department of Education's Web site to keep up with program offerings.
4. Survey the school staff to identify sources of previous grants to the school.
5. Identify contacts in the state education agency who can provide information about state (or state-administered federal) grant programs.
6. Conduct a staff development session on proposal writing. Enlist the aid of foundation staff plus school employees who have written previously funded proposals.
7. Visit the local Foundation Center Cooperating Collection Library.
8. Identify potential partners for grant requests.
9. Whenever a member of the staff plans on going to Washington, D.C., give them extra time and arrange meetings with program officers at federal agencies that might be potential funders for the school.

REFERENCE

AAFRC Trust for Philanthropy. (2000). *Total giving reaches $190.16 billion.* <http://www.aafrc.org>, July 21.

RESOURCES

The Foundation Center. (2000). *The Foundation Directory Online.* <http://www.fdncenter.org/subscribe2.html>, April 21.

The Foundation Center. (2000). *Foundation Finder.* <http://www.inp.fndcenter.org/finder.html>, April 21.

U.S. Department of Education. (2000). *Funding opportunities.* <http://www.ed.gov.funding.html>, April 21.

U.S. Department of Education. (2000). *Federal Register documents.* <http://www.ed.gov/legislation/FedRegister/>, July 21.

①

LOCAL MONEY SOURCES

Seeking discretionary funding support from local sources may not seen as exciting as soliciting grants from the government or large foundations, but it usually leads to a much higher percentage of success. Local may mean a private foundation in the state or region, a business located in the area, or individuals and organizations in the neighborhood or town.

A big advantage of local sources is that they are much more inclined to give on an ongoing basis or to give to projects that are not necessarily new or unique but that do benefit the community. The response time is generally much shorter when dealing with local organizations or individuals than with the government or major foundations. Usually, there is only one chance each year to receive money from federal government grant programs. Large foundations require at least a 90- or 120-day turnaround time. With local sources, it is not unusual to get a response in less than 30 days. In some cases, the response is immediate.

Local sources can be approached for small amounts. It is not efficient for the government or major national foundations to deal with requests in the hundreds of dollars or even a few thousand of dollars.

DEVELOPING LOCAL SOURCES

Prospecting for new sources of support can be done a number of ways:

1. *Upgrade previous contributors.* Any fund-raiser will say that the best prospect for new contributions to any cause are people or institutions that have contributed before. It is important to keep detailed records with dates, amounts, addresses, phone numbers, and any other relevant information to all previous contributors. This will become the base for future fund-raising efforts.

2. Obtain lists of past givers to related programs. Find out who in the school has been involved in other fund-raising campaigns. For example, someone may have raised money for the Boy Scouts or someone else for a local church youth group. People who have contributed to other youth organizations or to other educational institutions may be good prospects for supporting the school.

3. Get members of the staff, advisory groups, and parent organizations to think about personal contacts that may be beneficial in seeking external support. For example, provide lists of board of directors of local foundations and see who may have a relative or an acquaintance on the lists. Since many corporations make their philanthropic contributions in communities where their employees live, it is important to know who employs the parents of the students and who employs the students who work.

4. Develop the 5 percent and 2 percent clubs. As many businesses recognize their responsibilities as corporate citizens, these clubs have been established to honor those businesses that have contributed at least 5 percent or 2 percent of their gross profits to charitable causes. The Keystone Club in Minneapolis is an example of a group that annually cites corporations that make this commitment to the community. If this type of organization does not exist, work with other community leaders to provide this appropriate recognition for the better corporate citizens.

5. Seek support from those with vested interest in the school. An example of this are the various businesses that sell their products and services to school. This can be anyone from the local bakery or dairy that provides food for the lunch program to major publishers or computer manufacturers that provide equipment and materials for the curriculum.

6. Develop the school's own unique prospects. Use the following exercise with staff and advisory groups. Have each person take a sheet of paper. Ask each one to make a list of at least three names in each of the following categories: organizations of which you are a member, organizations in which you know any key person, bankers you know well, successful businesspeople you know, and wealthy retirees you know. Some people will list many names, and others will have few on their list. The names that will result provide the basis for expanding the number of potential sources for the school.

BUILDING THE SALES PITCH BOOK

The development of a fund-raising pitch book is necessary. This may be as simple as a one-page outline of talking points for those individuals who are going to be presenting the school's case to organizations or individuals. This pitch sheet or pitch book has all the elements of an informal grant proposal. Among the things to include are the following:

- *Information relating to the need for the program.* Facts concerning local and regional need are most persuasive, but if that type of data are not available, use state and federal information. For example, in developing a program to get more girls interested in science careers, there are national statistics that show this need even though there may be no local data on the subject. In some cases, if there is no evidence to support the specific need being addressed, use information that is available concerning related fields of interest.
- *The basic elements of the program.* This would include objectives, methods, personnel, and evaluation plans. These things do not need to be described as formally or in as much detail as in a grant application. They should be put in the appropriate language for the audience being addressed. Unlike a grant application, where everything must be in writing, the informal requests to local funders usually involve oral presentations with or without written statements. Because of this, it is possible to respond immediately to any requests, answer any questions, and be able to expand on any points that need clarifying.
- *Financial issues.* This includes the proposed budget and finance plans for the current project in continuation activities.
- *Why this is a good investment.* People like to believe that they are making wise investments with their money. This usually means that they expect a certain financial return, but when they are investing in a charitable activity, it should be explained that the investment will pay off in other ways:

1. Depending on the contributor's marginal rates on federal and state income taxes, one-third or more of the money will come from the government in reduced tax liability. Nothing is more satisfying to some people than to say where their money will go rather than having the government spend it for them.
2. The contribution will help meet a specific need. This approach would be used with those individuals who most want the project, for

example, when approaching parents of youth hockey players to support an indoor ice arena.

3. The money will be invested wisely and will be multiplied through contributed services, matching funds, and so forth. People who are frustrated with money leaving the community for what they feel are wasteful or inefficient programs of government and large nonprofit organization find this an attractive argument.

4. The contribution will help build a better community through the activity being funded. While appeals to community pride can be successful with individuals, they should have even more impact on civic and service organizations, such as a chamber of commerce, the Lions Club, the Kiwanis, and the Business and Professional Women's Organization.

5. The contribution enhances the giver's sense of self-worth. It is an investment that provides opportunities for people to feel good about themselves.

FACE-TO-FACE SOLICITATION

The most effective way to raise money is by direct face-to-face solicitation. There should be the greatest return and the lowest cost per contributor This can be done at home, at the office, or in a group situation. Getting volunteers to raise money this way is usually difficult at first, but once they experience success, it gets easier and more satisfying.

The way to make it easiest is in a group setting. Then solicitors really only have to bring someone to a meeting (at school or at some other public place, such as a restaurant or club), and one person can make the pitch to all contributors. The group setting can create an atmosphere where the members of the group influence one another to contribute. This is helped considerably if a few major contributors are lined up ahead of time to kick off the giving at the meeting.

Each worker should have a limited number of prospects to invite, usually not more than six or eight. One approach is to have a lunch meeting where workers agree to buy lunch for the ones they invite to their table. Thus, there are no direct costs except for the printed materials and pledge cards that are distributed.

Once the people are gathered and after time for casual conversation (or a meal), the key solicitor makes the pitch. Pledge cards should be available for everyone, and someone should be ready to collect the pledge card before people leave.

Group solicitation works best with groups that see themselves as peers. Local businesspeople, a social club, or members of a service group are examples. If a few members of the group make known their level of contribution, it may set a standard for the others.

It takes more effort to solicit individuals at home or at their place of business, but it can be very profitable. This requires training more people to make the fund-raising pitch and to devote more time to the effort.

Again, each worker should have a limited number of prospects. If asked to call on more than ten people, the inexperienced solicitor may find the task overwhelming. Also, if pledge cards are made up in advance, each worker should be given at least one or two certain contributors to start with. This will give them success and encourage them to continue if they get some turndowns later.

If at all possible, solicitors should be sent out in pairs. This will make it more likely that they will do the job and do it on time. It also means that if there are questions by the prospective donor, the team can work together in providing answers. Finally, the dual approach puts a little more pressure on the prospect if the two are his or her peers.

FUND-RAISING PHONE BANKS; OR, BOILER ROOM BASICS

Raising money by telephone is usually best done by a group of people working together in one location. This type of location is a phone bank, sometimes referred to as a "boiler room." In establishing a boiler room, a number of factors must be considered:

1. Cost. Telephone operations can be very expensive. It is important to keep fund-raising cost to a minimum. Use of school lines (outside of school hours) provides a phone bank at no cost, assuming that there are multiple lines in one location and the use of the phones will not interfere with other school business. Another option is to use phones donated by a business that has several telephones in one location, such as a brokerage house or real estate office. A third option is to make a nominal payment (e.g., $1 per line per night) to a business for use of the phones.

Schools should not pay commercial rates to have phones installed just for fund-raising purposes. The down payment required and the costs for use of lines would be far too great in relation to the money likely to be raised.

2. Location. The site should be easy to find, have adequate parking, and be accessible to handicapped. If the community has public transit, access to the system is important, especially for those too young to drive and for senior citizen volunteers. Finally, if phoning is to be done in the evening, the neigh-borhood must be safe and perceived so by the callers.

3. The room.   The room should provide a pleasant atmosphere. Provide a sign-in station for callers. To encourage workers, place both informative and motivational signs throughout the room. There should be no unnecessary noise or distractions. Food and beverages should be available, especially if phoning is to be done during the evening dinner hour. Make available adequate supplies and materials, such as lists, phone books, pencils, forms, envelopes, pledge cards, and so forth.

The workstations should be semiprivate. Individuals should have enough pri-vacy to get the work done, but there should be an opportunity for the supervi-sor to observe. An efficient operation should never have fewer than three phones per site.

4. Number of phones.   The number of phones needed is calculated by dividing the number of prospects by the number of shifts and dividing that result by the estimated number of calls an individual can *complete* each shift. For example, assume that 1,000 calls must be made in five days and that each caller can complete 25 calls in a shift. Dividing 1,000 (prospects) by 5 (shifts) means that 200 calls must be completed each shift. If each phoner is ex-pected to complete 25 calls, then there must be at least 8 (200 divided by 25) phones available.

If the number of phones available is inadequate, then the number of shifts must be increased. All these figures should be computed before the telephoning begins.

5. Prospecting.   Each caller must have lists to work from. The best prospects are previous contributors. Other prospect lists may include alumni, vendors, parents, neighbors, and friends of the school. It is important to collect lists from groups such as the adult education programs, booster clubs, civic or-ganizations, service clubs, and churches in the area. Everyone who has a rela-tionship with the school or who can be seen as a civic-minded person should be considered a prospect.

6. The callers.   The best callers are selected from employees, key groups that support the school, and others referred by either of those groups. For the calling program to succeed, there must be a cadre of activists to recruit other phoners and workers. This cadre must then set the standard for the others.

Provide training for the callers, including written instructions and scripts to use for the phone calls. It is very helpful to conduct a brief simulation of some calls. This will demonstrate the right way to conduct oneself, and it should put a newcomer at ease. School officials or key activists in charge of the program should be supervisors at the site to give encouragement, answer questions, and see that callers are performing in a positive and effective manner.

All callers should receive recognition. This should at least include an immediate thank-you followed by a letter or certificate of appreciation. Awards or prizes could be given for outstanding performance.

7. The call. Callers must project a pleasant attitude. "Keep a smile in the voice" is the phrase often used by professional trainers of telephone workers. The caller should follow a script, at least until secure in his or her own ability to make the call without help. Each caller should begin by calling the best prospects. This should lead to some success that will motivate the caller to continue. Usually, this means starting with previous contributors (if there are any), then prospects the caller knows personally, then referrals, and only then on to cold calls. Follow-up is crucial to successful phone bank fund-raising. Callers must continue to follow up on incomplete calls (busy signal or no response). A follow-up call may also be necessary when a prospect has raised objections or asked a question that the caller cannot answer. Callers must make note of any objections stated by prospects, whether they contributed or not.

8. The close. The caller must close the sale, that is, ask for a contribution. The caller must suggest an amount to be given, otherwise a potential $100 contributor may send in $5. After a successful call, get the informational materials and pledge cards out immediately. Also, obtain answers to any questions the contributor may have and give a response.

DIRECT-MAIL FUND-RAISING

Raising money by direct mail is usually not very efficient since a 5 percent return rate is considered very good. That means that for every 100 letters sent out, only five are returned. After calculating the cost of postage and printing and the time it takes to conduct the mailing, the net profit is far less than for other methods of raising money. Nevertheless, direct mail does have its uses, including trying to broaden the base of contributors to the school and/or combining a public relations effort with fund-raising.

Some basic tips for conducting a direct-mail campaign include the following:

1. Obtain lists. The most important lists to have are of all previous donors to the school. Those lists should have information that includes the size of the contribution, the date of the last contribution (even better to list the last three contributions, if available), the method of solicitation, and the relationship the individual has to the school.

Of vital importance to the success of a direct-mail campaign are the lists of new prospects. Heading these lists are referrals for previous donors followed by alumni, parents, staff, adviser groups, vendors, and any affiliated groups. Other lists that may be of value include contributors to other related causes (youth organizations, sports organizations, community groups, churches, and so forth) and contributors to similar schools.

2. Set goals and time tables.   Once the lists are compiled, it is important to estimate the number of contributors needed, the dollar amount to be raised, and the percentage of profit expected from the effort. Goals should also be set for groups solicited and contribution per individual. The first time a direct-mail campaign is conducted, these goals will be educated guesses. In subsequent campaigns, the goals can be realistically tied to past performance.

3. Develop the mailing package.   The three crucial elements to the mailing package are a brochure, a letter, and a return envelope with pledge card.

The brochure should be aimed at the individual contributor; it should provide a description of the school, the goals of the school, the specific purpose of this financial appeal, the benefits of contributing, and the value of the school to the community. The brochure should highlight the strengths of the school and be written so as to build a relationship with the potential contributors.

The letter should be personalized. Surprising as it may seem to the uninitiated, successful fund-raising letters are usually long. They include a number of specific appeals and several personal references to the contributor and to the group or groups to which the contributor belongs. It is important to add a P.S. at the end of the letter since this usually is read at a higher rate than anything else in the letter. Therefore, the P.S. should include a key appeal or the restatement of the most important appeal of the letter.

A return card and envelope should be included with each direct-mail piece. The return card should list a number of suggested contribution levels (e.g., $25, $50, and $100) and provide a space for another amount to be written in by the contributor. On the card should be a request for information on the contributor that would be useful to the school and a reminder that the contribution is tax deductible (unless the school is a for-profit organization). Since the rate of return will be low, it is usually far cheaper to use a "postage paid by addressee" imprint on the return envelope than to provide prestamped or metered envelopes.

4. Maintain data on all returns.   To determine the success of the fund-raising efforts and to lay the groundwork for future direct-mail appeals, detailed data should be kept. For each contributor, this should include name and address, the list the contributor was on, the field of interest, the date of the mailing, and the turnaround time between mailing and return.

General data collected should include total cost of the mailing, the number of pieces mailed, and the number of pieces returned and percentage return. Most important are the total dollar volume generated, the dollar average per return, and net profit from the mailing after expenses have been deducted.

5. Thank all contributors.   Promptness pays. Thank-you notes or cards should be sent to all contributors immediately. Some schools have different thank-you letters and certificates or awards based on the level of contribution. This should be determined before the first thank-you is mailed. Each thank-you should include a receipt for tax purposes.

6. Other issues. Those who do direct-mail solicitations find that the best contributors are those who have given in the past. This raises the question of how frequently these individuals can be solicited. The frequency of mailings should be determined by the needs of the school, the rate of return of previous mailings, and common sense. Political campaigns are so tuned in to the fact that previous contributors are the best prospects that they are solicited several times a year. Mailings that are too frequent can create negative reactions in previous supporters.

The direct-mail time tables should be integrated with other fund-raising activities. Since direct mail is usually the least efficient method of raising money, it should not be done before personal solicitation and telephone solicitation activities have ceased and should not interfere with fund-raising events. An exception to this is direct mail to first-time prospects who are not even on the lists for the other fund-raising activities.

It is important to determine whether the primary purpose of the direct mail is fund-raising or public relations. At times, the direct-mail campaign can be considered successful even if it loses money if the primary purpose was to inform people of the school's activities and programs.

Gimmicks are frequently used to try to increase the response to direct-mail campaigns. For example, people who usually throw out junk mail are more likely to open the envelope if it has a stamp rather than being metered. It is possible to get third-class stamps to place on the envelope. This increases the likelihood that the envelopes will be opened, which is the first step in getting a contribution.

Other gimmicks are sometimes used to increase the return rate or the dollar amount per contribution. For example, one solicitation placed in the envelope a pledge card that was torn in half. The letter began with a statement that sympathized with people being so tired of these kinds of solicitations that they are inclined to tear up the pledge card. After this attention-getting devise, the letter went on to explain the need. This technique led to a substantial increase in donations.

Some users of direct-mail fund-raising do not include return postage. Instead, they mention that by using their own stamps, the contributors are helping keep the cost down for the school.

FUND-RAISING EVENTS

Events can raise substantial amounts of money, or events can lose money. Events can energize a school, or events can demoralize a school. Events can bring great positive publicity, or they can be public relations disasters. If successfully done, fund-raising events can contribute greatly to the school, its economic well-being, its public image, and its community morale.

Events can be as simple as a student car wash on a Saturday afternoon and as complex as a weekend all-school fair that requires year-round planning. Because events are so varied, there is no one approach that will guarantee success, but there are some questions that need to be asked before an event is undertaken:

1. What is the purpose of the event? Is it fund-raising, publicity, community building, or something else? While there may be multiple purposes, if making money is the primary purpose, that should be made clear in the beginning.
2. How does the event fit in with other fund-raising activities? The event may undercut efforts at direct solicitation or confuse potential contributors if it is not coordinated with other revenue-raising activities.
3. Who will get the profits from the event? Does the school administration or the student government decide priorities for who gets to run fund-raisers, does all the money raised by the school go into a general fund with the profits to be distributed on a need basis, or is it every group for itself in moneymaking activities? What is the role of booster groups in find raising?
4. Is the event economically efficient? Does the amount of money raised justify the time and energy put into the event? Many times, schools get caught up in something such as magazine sales or candy sales when a less labor intensive effort might raise as much or more money.
5. Is there a budget? Will there be someone responsible to see that expenses do not get out of hand? Financial disasters with events are caused as much or more by overspending on expenses as by taking in too little revenue.
6. Are there people in the community who like to put on fund-raisers as their way of contributing to the school?

Once these questions are answered, running a fund-raiser is like any other project. There must be a plan with goals, a time line, and people with specific responsibilities.

PROFIT BY EFFECTIVE MANAGEMENT

Effective money management can easily lead to savings of 2 to 5 percent of an annual budget. Money management issues include paying bills, acquiring materials and equipment, obtaining professional services, building cash flow, collecting bills, investing, and the possible use of a foundation.

The first concern in money management is to know that funds are appropriately accounted for. Whenever there is a change in leadership in a school, an audit should be performed as soon as the new leadership takes charge. This protects the new leaders from any liability as a result of previous decisions made regarding the handling of funds. Even if an audit has been conducted, no matter how recently before a change in leadership, a new audit must be requested because control has been passed. Audits should then be conducted annually by an independent accounting firm.

Cash flow planning is crucial to the efficient operation of school. One of the most serious hidden costs for schools is short-term borrowing that frequently is a result of poor cash flow planning. Cash flow planning means plotting the timing and amounts of receipts and expenditures. In order to avoid short-term debt, it is necessary to start each fiscal year with enough cash on hand to carry the operation until significant revenue is received. The balance needed at the start of fiscal year will be determined by the anticipated flow of receipts and expenditures, particularly in the early part of the year.

Historically, it was recommended that public schools begin the fiscal year (typically July 1) with a balance equal to 20 percent or more of the annual operating budget in order to minimize financial problems during the year. With pressures from taxpayer groups on one side and employee organizations on the other, public schools today are fortunate if they can begin with a balance of 5 percent of the budget—a situation long familiar to private schools. New charter schools and other start-ups frequently have special problems in having enough money on hand to begin operations. They must be certain to have cash to make payrolls and other significant operating expenses until the income flow reaches a steady pattern.

Operating expenses are relatively easy to anticipate since the largest expenditures are in the area of salaries that are established before the year begins. Some expenditures, such as bills for energy consumption or snow removal, are more difficult to anticipate. They are usually based on the pattern of expenditures from previous years. Because of the uncertainty of these expenditures, it is helpful to estimate them on the high side.

For public schools, the primary sources of income are from state and local taxes. The dates and amounts of these receipts will be known at the beginning of the year. The only serious problem in estimating the revenue for a year will arise if the enrollment changes significantly. Enrollment forecasts should be done annually and should consider factors such as birth rates, migration rates, changes in attendance boundaries, and the opening or closing of schools in the market area. To help with long-range (five to ten years) planning, school officials should pay close attention to activities of real estate developers and municipal planning agencies.

Private schools have a greater challenge in forecasting revenue since the primary source is usually tuition (which may be supplemented by parish subsidies in parochial schools). The number of students and the level of tuition per student determine total tuition revenue. In estimating income, the school must always try to determine the point of diminishing returns when any tuition increases are proposed. This may require a survey of parents to see what level of increase could be enacted without a serious loss of enrollment. Complicating factors are sliding-scale tuitions based on need and/or tuition reductions for families with more than one student in the school. Private schools usually are dependent on fund-raising activities and possibly endowments as additional significant sources of revenue.

Examples of minor sources of revenue include such things as income from food service and vending machines, receipts from school activities, and student fees. These usually can be estimated from the patterns of previous years. For a new school, these can be estimated by using data from comparable schools.

TEN TIPS FOR GETTING THE MOST FOR THE MONEY

1. *Contract out any services that can be done more efficiently or more effectively by someone else.* Some schools long have contracted for nonacademic services, such as student transportation. There is a growing movement for school operators, including public school boards, to see themselves as *purchasers of services* rather than as *providers of service.* For each significant service, the question that should be asked is, How can we provide the highest-quality service at a reasonable cost?

   In addition to transportation, food service and building maintenance are areas that frequently have been outsourced. Other nonacademic areas, such as payroll and pupil and financial accounting, might easily be contracted out, allowing the school administration to focus on teaching and learning.

   The challenge for schools is to determine what professional services also might be done by contractors rather than by employees of the school board. Special services such as counseling, nursing, psychology, and social work might be provided by a private firm or by contract with a public entity (city, county, or intermediate education agency or another school district). The same could be true of a curriculum specialist or a consultant.

2. *Use formal bidding or informal quotes for all but the very smallest purchases.* Many units of government require a formal bidding process for purchases over a specific dollar amount, such as $10,000. They also require the taking of three or more informal bids for smaller amounts to a lower threshold, such as $1,000 or $2,000. The school should establish a policy on when to take bids, when to request quotes, and when to purchase products off the shelf. Even in public school systems, each school can set lower thresholds for bids and quotes than the law requires. Seeking formal bids for purchases over $1,000 and informal quotes from at least two or three vendors for purchases over $100 can produce significant savings for the school.

3. *Use group purchases whenever possible.* In some states, local units of government, such as schools and cities, are allowed to participate with the state government when purchasing material and equipment. These group purchases allow even small institutions to take advantage of quantity discounts. Where this is not possible, the school should consider forming agreements with other schools or nonprofit organizations to do joint purchasing.

4. *Be aware of the opportunity for prepayment discounts.* Even if discounts are not made available publicly, it never hurts to ask whether the vendor would give a discount for prepayment. This negotiation could save several percent off the price of purchase.

5. *Be aware of any penalties for late payments.* Make certain that payment deadlines are known and kept. There is no excuse for paying more than is necessary for products merely because of inattentiveness to payment schedules.

6. *Know which vendors allow long grace periods with no penalties for late payments.* It may be necessary to take advantage of this situation at those times when cash is in short supply.

7. *Be aware of surplus sales.* Government agencies sometimes sell used equipment at bargain prices to schools and nonprofit organizations. Corporations may also dispose of surplus furniture and equipment the same way. In some cases, corporations will give the equipment to schools, either for public relations purposes or because the tax benefits in giving the material away are more profitable than attempting to sell it to the public.

8. *Invest surplus cash in interest-bearing accounts, short-term certificates of deposit, or short-term Treasury bills.* Even a small school should be able to earn at least several hundred dollars a year by good financial planning. Determine those times of the year when there will be surplus cash on hand and invest the money until it is needed.

9. *Encourage members of the school community to shop at those businesses that have special programs for donating a portion of the sale price to the school.* Target department stores, for example, will donate 2 percent of each sale to the school of the purchaser's choice if the purchases are made with a Target Corporation charge card.

10. *Consider establishing an affinity credit card with one of the general credit cards, such as VISA or MasterCard.* While the percentage obtained on each purchase may be small, the total amount of money can add up if the members of the school community (employees, parents, and friends) use credit cards for most purchases.

A note of caution: Know which merchants are supporters of the school. It could be a serious mistake to save a few dollars on a single purchase by accepting a quote from a vendor who has no interest in the school and passing up the opportunity to do business with one who is a major contributor (of time, talent, or material resources) to the school. The same could be true of putting money in a remote bank to earn a few extra dollars while passing up a local bank that contributes regularly to the school and student organizations.

SUGGESTED ACTIVITIES

1. Survey the staff and supporters to see who has experience in fund-raising activities or events.
2. Review the fund-raising history of the school and the school-related organizations. Try to determine the relative benefit of each activity.
3. Conduct brainstorming sessions with students, staff, and supporters about possible fund-raising events.
4. Identify individuals who have played major roles or have been successful at direct solicitation for other causes, such as the United Way, church groups, or service and civic organizations.
5. Develop a detailed annual calendar of fund-raising activities.
6. Collect prospect lists and organize them by their special interests. For example, some would support athletics, others fine arts, and some the science program.
7. Determine who in the school has connections with local foundations, wealthy individuals, and organizations that might be prospects for financial support.
8. Examine the possible benefit of partnering with another school or organization in a fund-raising effort.

RESOURCES

American Fund Raising Institute, 7004 Comanche Drive, North Little Rock, Arkansas 72116. Telephone: 800-496-2374. Web: <http://www.afri.org>.

The Chronicle of Philanthropy, 1255 Twenty-third Street NW, Washington, D.C. 20037. Telephone: 202-466-1200. Web: <http://www.philanthropy.com>.

National Society of Fund Raising Executives, 1101 King Street, Suite 700, Alexandria, Virginia 22314. Telephone: 703-684-0410. Web: <http://www.nsfre.org>.

②

USE OF INTELLECTUAL PROPERTY

To promote the progress of science and useful arts, by securing for limited times to authors and inventors the exclusive right to their respective writings and discoveries.

—U.S. Constitution, Article I, Section 8

The term *intellectual property* refers to the results of effort to create new products, processes, materials, designs, or artistic or literary works. Most people earn a living by building products (e.g., working in manufacturing or skilled trades) or by providing services (e.g., education or health care). Other people earn their living by developing intellectual property, such as inventing new tools, discovering new medicines, writing books, producing movies, developing computer software, or composing music.

Schools could not function without the use of intellectual property. Books, newspapers, movies, videos, sheet music, software, works of art—all these are examples of intellectual property used daily in schools. This chapter presents a detailed discussion of what intellectual property is, ideas on how legally to make maximum use of other people's intellectual property at minimal cost to the school, and how the school can profit from the intellectual property as it develops.

TYPES OF INTELLECTUAL PROPERTY

Some basic understanding of the appropriate laws is necessary to use intellectual property effectively. Federal law protects three types of intellectual property: patents, trademarks, and copyrights. Patents are obtained and trademarks can be registered in the Patent and Trademark Office of the U.S. Department of Commerce. Copyrights may be registered with the U.S. Copyright Office in the Library of Congress.

A patent protects the rights of an inventor of a product or process. Patenting a product is a long and usually costly process. Businesses are willing to go through this process because once a patent is obtained, it gives the owner exclusive right to manufacture the product (or to license it to others) for at least seventeen years. Colleges, especially research universities and their faculty members, have made substantial profits from developing patented materials and products.

Elementary and secondary schools usually are not involved with patents because schools are not in the business of inventing products. The time and cost of getting a patent ordinarily would not be seen as an appropriate use of school resources. Even if it were possible to get a patent, the likelihood of making a profit would usually not be great.

A trademark is a word, phrase, symbol, or design or a combination of words, phrases, symbols, or designs that identifies and distinguishes the source of the goods or services of one party from those of others.

Trademarks are becoming important potential sources of income in higher-educational institutions. Colleges have established trademarks that enable them to make a profit on the sale of items such as T-shirts, coffee mugs, and posters. Most major universities known for either academic or athletic achievement are realizing multi-million-dollar profits from the use of their trademarks. Because of the success of the major institutions, many other colleges now are learning how to profit from their names.

Million-dollar profits are not likely for any elementary or high school, but it is possible to earn thousands of dollars of profit from sales of sweater, caps, T-shirts, and other items that display the school's logo or colors. In many communities, the school allows local merchants, at no cost, to sell goods that display the school's colors or logo.

In the spring of the year, it might be worthwhile for the school to convene a meeting with the local merchants informing them of the opportunity to sell goods displaying the school's trademarks. A reasonable fee should be negotiated for this right, with the fee to begin with the sale of goods for the following school year. The school could sell its own materials and make more money, but that would take far more effort and create possible public relations problems with the local vendors.

Vendor resistance to a licensing fee could cause the school marketing or public relations concerns that may outweigh the value of the financial profit from licensing its symbols. In that case, the school may be tempted to increase its visibility by encouraging everyone (student groups, businesses, booster clubs, and so forth) to freely produce products with the school's symbols. This approach worked well for the Grateful Dead, keeping that group's name in front of the public for years. Totally unrestrained permission probably would not be wise for a school since some thoughtless or devious parties might use the school logo or mascot in an inappropriate or offensive manner. If the licensing rights are not to be sold, the school should at least require a signed release for use.

The primary intellectual property issues for educators deal with copyright. The copyright protects the original artistic or literary work, including textbooks, computer software, multimedia educational products, and videotapes.

COPYRIGHT ISSUES

This section discusses the legal issues relating to copyright, gives suggestions on how to get the most effective use of other people's copyrighted materials, and discusses the considerations in developing one's own copyrighted materials.

The Copyright Act of 1976

Copyright is a form of protection provided by federal law to the authors of "original works of authorship," including literary, dramatic, musical, artistic, and other intellectual works. This protection is available to both published and unpublished works. Section 106 of the Copyright Act gives the owner of the copyright the exclusive right to do and authorize others to do the following things:

1. Reproduce the copyrighted works in copies or phonograph records
2. Prepare derivative works based on the copyrighted work
3. Distribute copies or phonograph records of the copyrighted work to the public by sale or other transfer of ownership or by rental, lease, or lending
4. Perform the copyrighted work publicly, in the case of literary, musical, dramatic, choreographic works, pantomimes, and motion pictures and other audiovisual works
5. Display the copyrighted work publicly, in the case of literary, musical, dramatic, and choreographic works, and pantomimes and pictorial, graphic, or sculptural works, including the individual images of a motion pictures or other audiovisual work
6. Perform the work publicly by means of a digital audio transmission, in the case of sound recordings.

The author of a work owns the copyright immediately at the time the work is created, but that right can be sold or given to others later. While it is not necessary to register a copyright, registration does establish a public record of the author's claim and is necessary before an infringement suit may be filed in court. Registration is a simple matter that requires submission of an application form to the copyright office, with the payment of filing fee ($20) and a copy (or copies) of the work being registered.

Section 107 of the Copyright Act deals with the fair use doctrine of copyright. The fair use provision recognizes the need to balance the rights of the owners of intellectual property with responsibilities of educational institutions and libraries to make information and creative works available to the public. Fair use allows reproduction in copies or recordings or by other means for criticism, comment, news reporting, teaching, scholarship, and research. The four factors in the fair use doctrine are the following:

1. The purpose and character of the use
2. The nature of the copyrighted work
3. The amount and substantiality of the portion used in relation to the copyrighted work as a whole
4. The effect of the use on the potential market for or value of the copyrighted work

Dialogue between organizations representing publishers, educators, and legislators led to very specific guidelines for the use of copyrighted materials in educational settings. Guidelines are available for print materials, music, and video recording. These guidelines should be kept in every school library or media center. If not available, they are easily obtained from the resources listed at the end of this chapter.

The discussion of the guidelines applies to books and periodicals. Single copies of the following may be made by a teacher for scholarly research or use in teaching or in preparation to teach: chapters from a book; articles from a periodical or newspaper; short stories, short essays, or short poems; and charts, graphs, diagrams, drawings, cartoons, or pictures from a book, periodical, or newspaper. Multiple copies may be made by the teacher for a course for classroom use or discussion (not to exceed more than one copy per pupil) according to these guidelines:

1. The copying meets the test of brevity as follows:
   • Poetry: a complete poem of less than 250 words or not more than two pages; for longer poems, an excerpt of not more than 250 words

- Prose: A complete article, story, or essay of less than 2,500 words or an excerpt of not more than 1,000 words, or 10 percent of the work, whichever is less
- Illustrations: one chart, graph, diagram, drawing, cartoon, or picture per book or periodical issue
- Special works: An excerpt of not more than two of the published pages and not containing more than 10 percent of the words found in the text

2. The copying is spontaneous. The copying must be at the inspiration of the teacher. The decision to use the work and the time for its use for maximum teaching effectiveness are so close that it is unreasonable to expect a timely reply to request for permission.

3. The copying meets the cumulative effect test as follows:
   - The copies are made for only one course
   - Only one short poem, article, story, or essay or two excerpts may be copied from the same author and not more than three from the same collective work or periodical volume during one class term
   - No more than nine instances of copying for one course during one class term

4. Each copy must include a notice of copyright.

These guidelines clearly prohibit certain activities. Copies are not to be used to create or substitute for anthologies, compilations, or collective works. No copies may be made from works that are intended to be consumable, such as workbooks or laboratory manuals. Copying may not substitute for purchase, be directed by a higher authority such as a principal or department head, and may not be repeated. Key factors in determining fair use are brevity, spontaneity in deciding to use the material, and the cumulative effect of the use of a variety of copyright materials during one class term. The same item cannot be copied by the same teacher from term to term. No charge should ever be made to students beyond the actual cost of copying.

Fair use means that copies can be made and used without prior approval of the copyright holder if the guidelines are followed. Some examples of appropriate use of fair use are as follows:

1. In preparing for a faculty meeting, the principal duplicates one article on discipline that she just read in the current issue of the *NASSP Bulletin*.
2. A social studies teacher tapes a television news report on campaign finance issues for use with his classes the next day.
3. An English teacher preparing a unit on poetry copies three short poems (less than 250 words each) by different authors as the basis for a class discussion.

4. On the weekend, the music teacher tapes a radio program on the history of jazz to be played as a part of Black History Month unit, which begins on Monday.

5. An art teacher copies one cartoon from each of several different magazines to show contrasting styles and detail in drawing.

In all these cases, the copies must include a notice of copyright. This is usually done by stating the source of the material, including publication date and author.

Some examples of serious copyright law violations by teachers are as follows:

1. *Copying from works intended to be consumable.* In science, a textbook is expected to last for seven years with a new accompanying lab manual to be used each year, so seven lab manuals should be sold during the life of each textbook. Since publishers base their estimates of income and expenses on this ratio, the principal who tells the science teachers to make copies of the lab manuals is illegally depriving the publisher of a fair return on its intellectual property.

2. *Using copied materials to create or substitute for anthologies, compilation, or collective works.* An English teacher who replaces a textbook by copying poems, short stories, plays, or major excerpts from novels clearly is violating the copyright unless permission has been granted for each of the materials used. Even with permission, copyrights may be violated if each copyright holder is not fully informed of the fact that the materials will be used to replace a text or anthology.

3. *Using videos for entertainment purposes as reward for good behaviors by the students.* The elementary school principal who rents a movie from the local video store to show to the student body the day before winter vacations is violating the fourth factor of fair use: the effect of the use on the potential market. If 500 students see the video in school, it reduces the likelihood of each of their families seeing the movie in a theater or purchasing the video themselves.

4. *Making a copy of computer software to install on another machine.* A teacher who sees a geography program on the computer when visiting another classroom and takes the software disk to install the program on his own machine is having an impact on the market for that product. Unless there is a site license or district license for the software, it can be used only on machines on which it was initially installed.

5. *Copying published sheet music for use in class.* Because of budget cuts, the principal eliminates the fund for the purchase of sheet music for the balance of the year. The choir director spends his own money to buy one copy of sheet music and then makes copies for the entire choir. Again, this is affecting the potential market for the work.

6. Copying puzzles from a current magazine for use with a class. An elementary school teacher decides that this is such good material that she will make extra copies to use with future classes. This violates the spontaneity provision of the fair use guidelines.

People frequently violate the copyright law. Some educators are apparently ignorant of the law, although any school with a competent librarian or media director should be aware of the major provisions that relate to schools. Other educators know that they are illegally copying materials but think that the law should not apply to them because they work for the government or a nonprofit organization or they feel that they are justified because they are helping children learn. Others violate the law because they believe that no one will know what they have done.

Cheaters are likely to get caught. Today, computerized inventory control can raise red flags that make it easy to determine when a school is violating copyright law by reproducing consumables. Sales personnel who visit school sites may see illegal copying. Parents who happen to work for a publisher or distributor of educational materials may notice illegal copies brought home from school by their own children.

TWELVE TIPS CONCERNING COPYRIGHT

1. *Plan ahead.* In order to obtain permission to use the best intellectual property available, curriculum planning should be done well in advance. This allows for the opportunity to receive permission and enables the school to develop alternative plans if permission is not granted.
2. *Develop and distribute to the entire staff forms to be used in seeking permission to use copyright materials.* Along with the forms should be a list of the most likely places teachers would submit requests, such as local newspapers, radio and television stations, professional educational organizations, national news magazines, television networks, and so forth. The list should include addresses, telephone numbers, fax numbers, and Internet addresses whenever possible. The easier it is to request permission, the more likely it is that requests will be made.
3. *Make no assumptions about which materials are copyrighted.* It is important to remember that since the passage of the 1976 Copyright Act, the copyright symbol (©) does not have to appear in copyrighted materials.
4. *Be careful about programs on public radio and television.* Educators often assume that because these are publicly supported institutions, their programming is in the public domain. That is not true. In fact, it is sometimes easier to get permission to use materials from commercial stations

than from public ones. Establish a relationship with the staff at the local news media so that permission is expedited when requests are necessary.

5. *Remember that everything in the newspaper is copyrighted.* Educators are sometimes confused because occasionally the byline for a story will say that the material is copyrighted by the writer. In that case, the writer has the copyright, but everything else in the paper is copyrighted by the publisher.

6. *Federal government documents are in the public domain and can be used without concern about copyright.* In most cases, documents of other units of government (states, cities, and counties) are also in the public domain, but there can be exceptions. Even if government documents are copyrighted, permission is usually granted for use.

7. *When rights must be purchased, seek reduced rates by group purchases rather than purchases by individual teacher or classrooms.* This is usually done in purchasing computer software in which the school can seek a site license to put the software on all computers in the building. A school district or association of schools can seek a group license for all computers under its jurisdiction.

8. *Rent videos and films from organizations that have paid the copyright fees.* The safest way to use videos and films is to rent them from an organization, such as a university or state distribution service, that has paid the appropriate copyright fees and built that into the rental costs.

9. *Seek the use of nonroyalty plays when mounting theatrical productions for limited audiences.* One of the few areas in which schools historically have paid appropriate fees is in the area of theater, in which royalties must be paid in order to produce well-known plays. If the school's theater activities are not major moneymakers and the production is primarily for educational purposes, reduce operating costs by using nonroyalty plays.

10. *Purchase generic music for use with student creative arts projects.* Music can greatly enrich a student-produced video or multimedia program, but most music licensing fees would be too costly for a school. Included in the price of "off the shelf" generic music is the license to use it in any way desired, entirely or in part, including public performance, without the payment of additional fees.

11. *Use public domain materials whenever possible.* In a general music class, the songs of Stephen Foster or other nineteenth-century composers can be used just as effectively as more recent music. It is important to remember that even though the music may be in the public domain, a specific arrangement may be copyrighted.

12. *Be wary of using materials from the Internet.* The newness and rapid growth of this medium raises many concerns, including accuracy of information and intellectual property issues.

CREATING INTELLECTUAL PROPERTY IN THE SCHOOL

Schools are not usually thought of as creators of intellectual property in the sense that schools historically have not been in the business of seeking a financial profit from their creations. School logos and songs are examples of creations of the school that have been freely used by one and all.

Of greater importance is the issue of who profits from academic material developed in the school, such as textbooks, software, videotapes, and multimedia productions. This is becoming a more complex issue as schools move from textbook-based curricula to project-based programs.

Creating intellectual property in the school can be satisfying and profitable, but there are some pitfalls to be avoided. Who owns the material that is developed and used in the classroom? For example, if a teacher develops some popular software for use in classes, the school usually is considered the owner of the software since it was created as part of the job. For the teacher to claim ownership, he or she may have to prove that it was developed out of school, on the teacher's own time, and using the teacher's home computer and that the development was not an expectation of employment.

To prevent acrimony and to build a sense of partnership, the school should establish a policy of ownership of intellectual property that will make winners of everyone. The policy might state that teachers will be encouraged to develop projects and material as part of their jobs with the understanding that any profits, after deduction of reasonable expenses, would be divided between the teacher and the school. The details of the agreement should be spelled out in a written contract that is understood by all parties, including the school board, before beginning any concerted efforts to develop materials.

Production could include everything from computer software to videotapes. Of particular use in the classroom would be learning packages or units that could be used to develop and demonstrate student competencies in the various curricular areas.

A plan must be made for how to best profit from materials developed. Some options are as follows:

1. The school will market the materials, although most schools are not prepared to do that effectively.

2. The school could sell the copyright to a commercial publisher or producer, retaining the right to continue to use the material.
3. The school could develop licensing agreements with other schools or with publishers.
4. The school could sell its rights to the teachers who developed the property and let the teachers market it themselves.

Another practical option would be for the school to enter into an arrangement with other schools so that each would have free access to any materials developed by members of the cooperative group. The cooperative then might sell or license rights to outside groups if the material has broad appeal. This type of cooperative probably would work best if schools with different curricular strengths (e.g., one strong in the sciences pairing with one strong in the humanities) banded together to develop a variety of products that none of the schools could afford to do alone.

SUGGESTED ACTIVITIES

1. Check the Library of Congress's Web site for changes or new information on copyright law. This should be done annually.
2. Develop a standard form for requesting permission to use copyrighted materials. Distribute copies of the form to all faculty members.
3. Meet with local news media (newspaper, radio, and broadcast television) seeking broader permission and/or an expedited process for the use of materials in school. (e.g., permission to save taped footage from a newscast for use in more than one school term).
4. Meet with local cable television providers to get their materials concerning the use of cable programs in school, such as Cable in the Classroom, a public service of the cable television industry.
5. Conduct a staff development meeting on how to use the fair use doctrine effectively. Training on the basics of copyright law must be done first.
6. Seek site licenses for all software regularly used in the school.
7. Provide teachers with lists of sources of movie and video rental services whose fees include the right to use copyrighted materials, public domain materials, generic music, nonroyalty plays, and any other material that can be freely used in the school.
8. Develop standards for the presentation and use of the school's logos, colors, and mascot. Register them with the Patent and Trademark Office and then determine whether to license or sell products using the logos.

9. Conduct brainstorming sessions on creating educational intellectual property at school and develop agreements concerning institutional and individual rights for materials developed.
10. Meet with other schools about forming intellectual property reciprocal agreements or partnerships.

RESOURCES

Franklin Pierce Law Center (basic intellectual property information), 2 White Street, Concord, New Hampshire 03301. Telephone: 603-228-1541. Web: <http://www.fplc. edu/tfield/ipbasics.htm>.

U.S. Copyright Office, Library of Congress, 101 Independence Avenue, Washington, D.C. 20559-6000. Telephone: 202-707-3000. Web: <http://www.loc.gov/copyright>.

U.S. Patent and Trademark Office, Crystal Plaza 3, Room 2C02, Washington, D.C. 20231. Telephone: 800-786-9199. Web: <http://www.uspto.gov>.

INDEX

ABOUT THE AUTHORS

Dr. Robert J. Brown is professor of educational leadership at the University of St. Thomas in St. Paul, Minnesota. Brown sees education from several perspectives, having been a state senator, a member of the Minnesota State Board of Education, a special assistant to the U.S. secretary of education, and the Scholar in Residence with the National Association of Secondary School Principals. He has over thirty-five years of experience in education policy and training school administrators.

Dr. Jeffrey R. Cornwall holds the Sandra Schultz Endowed Chair in Entrepreneurship at the University of St. Thomas in St. Paul, Minnesota. He was the founder, president, and CEO of Atlantic Health Systems, which provided a full continuum of health programs, including state-licensed private schools. Cornwall has written and presented extensively on entrepreneurship in business, and consults regularly with profit and nonprofit organizations. He has also taught at the University of Wisconsin, Oshkosh, and the University of Kentucky.